COWBOY MOVIES
&AMERICAN CULTURE

UNDERSTANDING THE INVASION OF IRAQ

PATRICK O'NEIL

Wholesale discounts for book orders are available through Ingram or Spring Arbor Distributors.

ISBN

978-1-77302-045-7 (paperback)

978-1-77302-046-4 (hardcover)

978-1-77302-047-1 (ebook)

Published in Canada.

First Edition

TABLE OF CONTENTS

Dedication vi

Preface vii

Chapter 1 — Changing World Opinion 1

Chapter 2 — A Penchant for Prevarication. 17

Chapter 3 — The Influence of Cowboy Culture in America Today. 55

Chapter 4 — Violence in America: Inherited from Cowboy Culture 69

Chapter 5 — Good vs. Evil: The Bush Mentality. 83

Chapter 6 — Manipulating and Abusing International Law 103

Chapter 7 — Revenge Drives the Violence 125

Chapter 8 — Money: The Predominant Goal in America. 135

Chapter 9 — The Fallout from Iraq: Will It Be Nuclear?. 145

Chapter 10 — Is George Bush a Real Cowboy? 153

Conclusion. 161

Reference Texts. 167

Notes 169

"In this fact-filled, thought-provoking book, Patrick O'Neil takes the reader to the roots of the 2003 American invasion of Iraq. His analysis reveals how the "artificial cowboy", George W. Bush, was inspired by the mythology of America's cowboy heroes as depicted in the American myth factory, Hollywood. O'Neil interweaves politics and culture to leave us in agreement as to the incompetence and immorality of Bush's predatory invasion of Iraq."

— LORRAINE MELTZER

"Patrick O'Neil gives the reader a creative and insightful look at George W. Bush's blood-thirsty invasion of Iraq in 2003. This book reveals how the cowboy president, aided and abetted by the sycophantic media, constantly lied to and betrayed the American people as he led his country into a war that was illegal, unnecessary and immoral."

— COLLEEN MOIR

"Patrick O'Neil is crisp with his language and clear with his facts in expertly highlighting Bush's descent into the hell that he created in Iraq. This book stitches together all of the astounding lies, deceptions and warped thinking on the part of Bush and his gang of outlaw cowboys in the White House. Focusing on the greedy and malicious foreign policy that led to this debacle of a war, O'Neil creates a detailed and thought-provoking analogy, linking traditional cowboy values to the ultimate rationale for the illegal invasion of Iraq."

— BRYON DOHERTY

"I like this book! George W. Bush got away with murder when he launched his illegal invasion of Iraq, and someone needed to hold his feet to the fire. O'Neil's book gives us yet another vision of the pervasive nightmare influence of the military-industrial complex in America, and the billions of tax-payer dollars wasted on this outrageous excuse for a war."

— BARBARA PEABODY

DEDICATION

To my wonderful children Shannon, Kelly and Kit and especially for that super-athlete and VIP in my life, my granddaughter Xenia.

PREFACE

It is common knowledge now that the Bush regime used a complex web of lies and deceit to lead America into the debacle that was the invasion of Iraq. All of the reasons given for war at the time of the invasion were not true, including weapons of mass destruction, the phantom connection between Iraq and al Qaeda, Iraq being a sponsor of the 9/11 attack, Iraq being a perpetrator of world-wide terrorism, the promotion of democracy in the Middle East or the need for 'regime change'. Critics since then have focussed on the need for America to capture Iraqi oil, and on the ability of Dick Cheney to manipulate and control George W. Bush in order to achieve his goal of global hegemony. While these reasons may define in a macroscopic way America's true rationale for this predatory invasion, a more microscopic view of George W. Bush as the self-described "decider" in the White House defines the true nature of why he was so easily manipulated by the neocon war hawks who had him surrounded in the Oval Office. We can come to a true understanding of what motivated George Bush to allow himself to be manipulated into invading Iraq by examining his self-proclaimed image as a cowboy, and by examining the values and principles inherent in that legendary character who rode out of the American West.

The evocative image of the American cowboy has over the past 150 years transitioned in the United States into an important symbol of what it means to be an American. The mythological cowboys of the 'Old West' were strong, steadfast and resolute, performing acts of courage and bravery while standing up to the forces of evil. Like the knights of King Arthur's court, the legendary cowboy has become a symbol to most Americans of what makes their country great, and today in America the rodeo cowboy, the urban cowboy, the cowboy of country and western music and especially the Hollywood cowboy have synthesized into an American icon, symbolizing some of the most important values that Americans hold close to their hearts.

Over the last few years, two American presidents have exemplified that contemporary cowboy image. Like Ronald Reagan before him, George W. Bush encouraged his public image as the "cowboy president", adopting the paraphernalia, the hackneyed clichés, the strut and the Texas drawl of the traditional American cowboy. More ominously, President Bush also carried with him the values inherent in that image, values that are replicated in most cowboy movies made in Hollywood over the past 100 years. It was these values that motivated George W. Bush between February, 2001 and March, 2003 as he created the momentum in America that led to the invasion and destruction of the sovereign nation of Iraq.

Leonard Cohen in his song <u>Democracy</u> called America "the cradle of the best and the worst", and we see that dichotomy repeatedly as America interacts with the world. America was at its very best when its military helped the Allies defeat the Nazis and Japan in World War Two. America was at its best when it helped establish a framework for international law after World War Two, through its support for the Nuremburg Protocols, the Geneva Conventions and the charter of the United Nations. America is at its very best when it shares with the world its wealth, its many scientific inventions, its literature, its music, its athletes and its cinema. But America is at its very worst when its hi-tech military uses its war machine and its toxic chemicals to cause death and destruction in so many countries around the world. An estimated two million Vietnamese died in that terrible military disaster in the 60's and 70's, just one of many nations that have suffered armed intervention at the hands of the USA. An article in the Washington Post on October 24th, 1965 quoted a Vietcong officer as saying to his American prisoner, "You were our heroes after World War Two. We read American books and saw American films, and a common phrase in those days was 'to be as rich and as wise as an American'. What happened?"

That same question was asked by many highly-respected political and military observers from around the world, and from America itself, after the invasion of Iraq. What happened to the United States of America, a country that many considered a bastion of democracy, so that it would in complete violation of its democratic principles attack a sovereign nation that was at no time a threat to the United States?

According to a Cost of War project by Brown University, updated on April 15, 2016, the war in Iraq has cost America $4.4 trillion, while creating 7.6 million war refugees and displaced persons. Brown University calculations put the death total for innocent civilians in Iraq at over 210,000. **1.** Ali Soufan was a member of the FBI during the 9/11 terrorist attacks, but left the FBI to form his own research company, called The Soufan Group. In 2015 his company released statistics showing that 1.2 million Iraqis died as a result of the invasion perpetrated by George W. Bush. The astronomical number of widows and orphans in Iraq is a cruel testament to a president who put cowboy values and crass brutality ahead of respect for human life, a blatant contradiction of his Christian values. Virtually the entire infrastructure of Iraq was destroyed, as innocent civilians tried desperately to survive with no clean water, bombed-out hospitals, little food, schools destroyed, with no electricity, many of its mosques targeted and the constant, daily bombardment of murderous technological weaponry.

Hollywood reveals much about America, including both the ominous culture of military conflict that has left that country in a constant state of war for over one hundred years, and the persistent cowboy culture of the Old West that has seen cowboy values become an inherent part of American culture today. Most of the war movies about Vietnam released in the years following that war were based on true stories and detailed outrageous atrocities. Platoon, Casualties of War, Full Metal Jacket and Apocalypse Now showed a descent into darkness that was truly diabolical. In the same way that Hollywood helped define Vietnam, movies have also helped bring the invasion of Iraq into focus. However, it is not exercises in patriotic propaganda like The Hurt Locker or American Sniper that shed light on the war in Iraq. Instead, it is the values predominant in cowboy movies that explain why America engaged in this illegal war. The continued presence of so many cowboy movies in American theaters over the years has promoted cowboy values to become an inherent part of American culture, thus explaining among other values the blood-drenched gun culture prevalent in America today. While defining the public persona of the enigmatic cowboy President, George W. Bush, cowboy movies have also provided a concise frame of reference for why he launched his predatory war.

America's potential to be a positive and progressive influence in the world is reflected in its many world-famous historical characters, including Walt

Disney and Walt Whitman, Thomas Jefferson and Thomas Edison, Benjamin Franklin and Frank Lloyd Wright. America can recapture the respect of the rest of the world, because it has proven time and again that it has the right stuff, and is incredibly resilient. Alexis De Tocqueville came from France in 1831 to tour America and in 1835 he published a book about this fledgling democracy. Titled "On Democracy in America", his book had an immediate impact both in Europe and in the USA. Even today it is on the prescribed reading lists of many famous universities, among them Princeton, Oxford and Cambridge. In one of his many cryptic observations about America and its continuing quest to be great, De Tocqueville said, "America is great because it is good. If America ever ceases to be good, it will cease to be great".

The United States under George W. Bush made the transition that de Tocqueville referred to, with the invasion of Iraq, ceasing to be good as it embraced the outlaw culture of the cowboy villains of old. Cowboy culture has had a pervasive influence on American culture for many years, and in 2003 George Bush rode his cowboy values into Iraq and in the process contradicted all that was good in the image of the traditional American cowboy.

This book details the scope and influence of cowboy culture in America, and outlines how the cowboy President, inspired by his incipient cowboy principles, launched this illegal war, and brought death and destruction to a country that was never at any time a threat to the United States. By examining five of the most popular cowboy movies from the past fifty years, and the five predominant values that drive the plot of each movie, we can come to a true understanding of the rationale for invading Iraq. Playing the role of the cowboy, at a time when the traditional cowboy has virtually disappeared from the American landscape, George W. Bush started an explosion of violence that still today, almost 13 years later, seems to have no end in sight. Many astute observers have predicted that the next world war, if there is one, would start in the Middle East. Now that Russia has joined America, Iran and 62 other countries in the fighting against the Islamic State in Iraq and Syria, and with 42 terrorist groups from around the world expressing support for ISIS, this very scary scenario, created and produced by George W. Bush, could potentially evolve into a very deadly and destructive world war.

CHAPTER 1

CHANGING WORLD OPINION

"There has never been a good war or a bad peace."

— BENJAMIN FRANKLIN

The United States of America was a nation of heroes after World War Two. People from virtually every country admired and respected Americans for the role that they played in that war. The goodwill, the credibility and the respect for America stretched around the world, and only increased with world-wide exposure to American culture, including its athletes, novels, music and movies. Cowboy movies in particular portrayed Americans as heroic, valiant, courageous and righteous, and people of many nationalities around the world saw Americans in the same light.

This credibility took a serious hit with the war in Vietnam, for no one liked to see the neighborhood bully beat up on a small, impoverished, 3rd world country. In the weeks and months immediately following the high-jacked airliners of 9/11 and the terrorist attacks on the twin towers, the United States witnessed a distinct revival of international solidarity, friendship and compassion. The USA received more offers of assistance and support from around the world, after that gruesome attack, than at any time in its history. In just one of many examples, in Gander, Newfoundland, Canadians opened their hearts and their homes to the many American travelers stranded at the Gander airport because subsequent to 9/11 the skies of America had been closed to all air traffic. International flights destined for American cities on the east coast were diverted to Gander, and its runways were lined with 747's full of passengers. There was not nearly the number of hotel or motel rooms in the small town of Gander to accommodate even a fraction of their number. Without hesitation, the residents of Gander took all of the passengers into their homes, fed them, gave them a bed to sleep in, and took care of them, until such time as they were able to continue on to their ultimate destination. Lifelong friendships developed from the bond that was created from that emergency situation. Canadians from across the country also volunteered to go to New York and assist in any way they could to help America recover from that terrible tragedy. There were so many Canadians volunteering to assist that many had to be turned away. The American national anthem could be heard at historic sights all over the world following 9/11, including at Buckingham Palace in London, at Brandenburg Gates in Germany and at the Palace at Versailles in France.

Less than two years after 9/11, this compassion was considerably less pronounced, as world opinion turned against the USA. By late 2003, America was identified by the majority of those polled world-wide as the single greatest threat to world peace. In Indonesia, which has the largest Muslim population in the world, over 75% of the people polled in 2002 had a favorable impression of the United States. A year later a similar poll showed that less than 15% of the population had a favorable impression of the USA. **1.** This represents a significant and very negative change in opinion, and that change in opinion was mirrored in Europe and around the world. American Arthur Schlesinger, a former Kennedy advisor, author and historian, said "the global wave of sympathy that engulfed the United States after 9/11 has given way to a global wave of hatred of American arrogance and militarism". He went on to say that the public regarded George Bush as a greater threat to world peace than Saddam Hussein. **2.**

This transformation in world-wide attitudes towards America came about because of the invasion of Iraq. But more particularly it came about because there has never been a believable or justifiable explanation from the White House as to why this illegal war was ever necessary. The manipulative regime members in Bush's cabinet who perpetrated this assault cast about from one prevarication to another as they struggled to justify the slaughter of 210,000 innocent Iraqi civilians. To paraphrase Howard Zinn, professor of political science at Boston University and author of over 20 books on a variety of political topics, there is no flag large enough to cover the shame of killing so many innocent civilians in Iraq.

In the midst of this carnage, every rationale for the war that the Bush regime promoted was proven to be false. Intelligent observers from around the world tried to understand why America would squander with such reckless abandon the alliances, the good will and the support that had been generated by that abominable 9/11 attack on America, just as they struggled to understand the many deceptions used by the Bush regime members to dupe and ultimately betray the people of the United States. There were no weapons of mass destruction, there was no connection between Saddam Hussein and al Qaeda, Iraq played no role whatsoever in the 9/11 attacks and Iraq was never a propagator of world-wide terrorism.

More than thirteen years after America's invasion, and despite the fact that this war was launched to curtail terrorism, Iraq continues to be overwhelmed by a veritable maelstrom of terrorist violence that seemingly has no end. The Islamic State of Iraq and Syria (ISIS), an off-spring of al Qaeda but now alienated from that terrorist organization, is perpetrating its own brand of death and destruction, beheading any foreigner that can be kidnapped, and capturing wide swaths of land in Iraq and Syria. ISIS had its beginnings in 1999 as Jama'at al-Tawhid wal-Jihad and was led by a Jordanian, Abu Musab al Zarqawi. The most infamous terrorist attack sponsored by this group was the 2003 bombing of the UN building in Bagdad that left 34 dead and many wounded. Zarqawi stated that the attack on the U.N. was in retaliation for the U.N. giving Palestine to the Jews, "so that they could rape the land and humiliate our people." 3. Zarqawi became a terrorist megastar thanks to the fabricated address that Colin Powell gave to the U.N Security Council on Feb. 3, 2003. In his address, Powell stated.

"Iraq today harbors a deadly terrorist network headed by Abu Musab al-Zarqawi, an associate and collaborator of Osama bin Laden. The Zarqawi network helped establish another poison and explosive training center camp. This camp is located in northeastern Iraq. From his terrorist network in Iraq, Zarqawi can direct his network in the Middle East and beyond. They have now been operating freely in the capital for over eight months." 4.

Rather than exposing an al Qaeda leader, Powell in fact was creating one, because most of what Powell said in that address was untrue. Zarqawi was not a member of Al Qaeda at that time, and was not even in Iraq in 2002. There were no Al Qaeda affiliates in Iraq, nor was Zarqawi running a terrorist network there. The whole story was invented by the Bush administration in order to provide justification for the invasion of Iraq. It was specifically because of Powell's lies, foisted on him by Bush and Cheney, which caused Zarqawi to gain prominence within the terrorist underground that evolved in Iraq after the American invasion in March of 2003.

Zarqawi was responsible for the first publicized beheadings by the group that later became ISIS, dressing American captives Nick Berg and Eugene Armstrong in orange jumpsuits, in imitation of the Muslim captives at Guantanamo, and then cutting their heads off while filming the whole disgusting event on video. This was done in retaliation for the horrors at Abu Ghraib prison. Zarqawi, a Sunni, later attempted to start a civil war between Sunnis and Shiites. His group affiliated with al Qaeda in 2004 and changed its name to al Qaeda in Iraq (AQI). In June of 2006 Zarqawi was killed by an American attack on a "safe house" and Abu Abdullah al-Bagdadi became the new leader of AQI. The American military sponsored a "surge" in 2006-2007 and AQI was chased across the border into Syria. In 2010 AQI leader Abdullah and another leader al Masri were killed in the fighting and Abu Bakr al-Bagdadi became the new leader. It was at this point that AQI became ISIS, with its stated aims of monotheism and Holy War.

ISIS is in effect trying to form a "caliphate", a distinct geographic area in the Middle East with a political identity that adheres to the traditional form of Islam going back 1300 years. This group now claims religious, political and military authority over all Muslims worldwide. Their goal of establishing a "caliphate" was one of the long-term goals of Osama bin Laden and al Qaeda, although bin Laden didn't expect this concept to develop so quickly. With funding provided by the oil money from Qatar and Saudi Arabia, ISIS moved back into Iraq in 2014 and quickly defeated an American-trained Iraqi army that was over ten times its size and far better equipped. ISIS seized their abandoned weapons as the Iraqi army fled in disarray, and then plundered Iraqi banks to the tune of almost $1.5 billion. ISIS took control of 1/3 of Iraq, including several lucrative oil fields, and began selling Iraqi oil on the black market to finance its atrocities.

Amnesty International has accused ISIS of "ethnic cleansing of historic proportions" and the United Nations has formally declared ISIS a "terrorist organization". There are currently 65 countries waging war against ISIS in the Middle East, and recent headlines in the Vancouver Sun, among many other media outlets, speak to the ominous involvement of so many countries in this conflict. On October 8th, the Sun cautioned "Russian Missiles Raise the Stakes" and on October 9th the headline read "Russian Action Irks Turkey". In one of the most startling events of this war, on November 24, 2015 Turkey showed just how much it was "irked" by shooting down a Russian SU-24 military jet when it flew over Turkish territory, killing one of the pilots. Turkey, which is a member of NATO and supposedly a strong ally of the USA in its fight against ISIS, is bombing the Kurds, who are also allies of the USA and are carrying the ground war against ISIS. Russia entered this conflict supposedly to help in the fight against ISIS, but instead has been bombing rebel groups trying to overthrow Assad in Syria. Meanwhile, ISIS (no longer affiliated with al Qaeda) and the Nusra Front (an al Qaeda affiliate) are both fighting Assad in Syria, but also have been fighting each other. Saudi Arabia is supposedly a staunch US ally, but refuses to enter the war against ISIS and it is believed that most of the funding for ISIS is coming underground from Saudi sources. These various conflicts underline how this war could go sideways in a very big hurry.

Despite the involvement of so many countries fighting ISIS, a current article on Yahoo News quoted a British soldier who had fought in Iraq as saying that ISIS could never be defeated militarily. Every bomb that is dropped in the Middle East creates more new terrorists, both there and around the world. Alexis de Tocqueville commented on this quagmire 180 years ago when he said, "There are two things which a democratic people will always find very difficult- to begin a war and to end one." George Bush told us that hostilities had ended when he landed in his Top Gun uniform on USS Kittyhawk in

2003, but in fact the war had just begun at that time, and it is still in play 13 years later.

On December 11, 2014 The Guardian's Martin Chulov interviewed a senior leader of ISIS, one who came up through the ranks with the group's top leader, Abu Bakr al-Baghdadi. The single most interesting quote from the ISIS leader gives a clear perspective on the effect of the American invasion. Bakr al-Baghdadi credits the group's rise in large part to American prison camps during the Iraq war, which he says gave him and other jihadist leaders an invaluable forum to meet one another and to plan their later rise. The ISIS leader said, "Seventeen of the twenty-five most important Islamic State leaders running the war in Iraq and Syria spent time in US prisons between 2004 and 2011." 5. ISIS is in fact a creation of the American prison system and the current onslaught of terrorism in Iraq emanated directly from the U.S. invasion. Former U.S. Ambassador to Iraq James Jeffrey exclaimed, as ISIS was easily defeating Iraq's American-trained army, "We're in a goddamn freefall here! This thing is going to degenerate into a regional cataclysm." Rather than attacking and defeating terrorism, Bush with his invasion of Iraq has in fact encouraged and enhanced the terrorist presence in that country.

Saddam Hussein was a Sunni Muslim, and throughout the Middle East Sunni and Shiite factions have been in conflict for many years. The devastating war between Iraq and Iran in the 1980's was in part a result of animosity between Shiites and Sunnis, with the leadership in Iraq being Sunni and Iran being predominantly Shiite. Strange as it may seem, Iran is now fighting ISIS in Iraq, in concert with the USA, in order to help bolster the Shiite government in Bagdad, despite years of animosity between the USA and Iran. Meanwhile, many disaffected Sunnis who have been shut out of the predominantly Shiite government in Baghdad are quick to join ISIS, for its leaders and many of its fighters are the remnants of Saddam's decommissioned army. One of the many criticisms of the Bush invasion was that the Iraqi army was not kept intact and co-opted, to help with the transition to a new government. By disbanding the army, and firing anyone with a government job who belonged to the Baathe Party, Bush created an instant insurgency, and laid the groundwork for the violent expansion later on of the ISIS ideology. Disbanding the army was also an indirect cause of the national library being burned to the ground, and the invaluable museums being looted. On direct orders from the Pentagon,

American soldiers were zealously guarding the oil ministry offices, while allowing national treasures in Bagdad to be stolen, burned or trashed.

Iraq lost much of its wealth and culture in this mundane war, but this seems to be but a footnote in history. More than half of all national archaeological sites, including the major Sumerian ones, were destroyed by the war. Massive looting at the National Museum in Bagdad saw the disappearance of over 15,000 of the 20,000 artifacts on display. This was a catastrophic loss not just to Iraq but to the entire world. Some of these artifacts on display were over 7000 years old, the oldest antiquities in the world. Said Macguire Gibson, president of the American Academic Research Institute, "It is a tragedy not experienced since the Mongol invasion."

For 1200 years Bagdad was considered the most refined, civilized and cultured city in the world. 12,000 years ago, Iraqis invented irrigated farming systems. They invented writing, founded modern mathematics, were the first culture to tell time, and were using Pythagoras' theorem 1700 years before Pythagoras. They established the first legal system that protected the weaker members of society, including widows, orphans and the disabled. They were the first civilization to build cities and live in them. For thousands of years they were the only culture that wrote poetry, history and "sagas". They were the first great horse-breeders and became the first to use cavalry as part of their military. That the American soldiers rushed to protect Iraq's oil ministry offices, but left Iraq's precious museums and heritage sites to be looted and trashed, speaks volumes about the priorities, the values and the sensitivity of the Bush regime. It also speaks to the devastating ignorance of the neocons in the White house in regard to Iraqi history and culture.

In July 2005, Britain's Royal Institute of International Affairs released a study repeating the conclusions of intelligence agencies around the world:

"There is no doubt that the invasion of Iraq has given a boost to the al-Qaeda network in propaganda, recruitment and fundraising, while providing an ideal training area for terrorists."

This comes as no surprise. Before Iraq was ever invaded, the National Intelligence Council in the United States predicted that "an American-led invasion of Iraq would increase support for political Islam and would result in a deeply divided Iraqi society prone to violent internal conflict." **6.**

In 2007, <u>Newsweek</u>'s Mike Isikoff reported:

"Ex-CIA operative Henry Compton told <u>Newsweek</u> that a world-wide surge in Islamic radicalism has worsened recently, increasing the number of potential terrorists and setting back U.S. efforts in the terror war. 'Certainly we haven't made any progress,' said Compton. 'In fact we've lost ground.' He cites Iraq as a factor; the war has fueled resentment against the United States." **7.** At the same time that America is fighting ISIS in Iraq and Syria, supposedly in concert with the Shiite government in Bagdad, Shiite militias have been attacking and kidnapping Americans in Iraq, just one of many anomalies in this conflict.

Before the invasion of Iraq, Egypt's Hosni Mubarek said, "Today you have one Osama Bin Laden to deal with. If you invade Iraq you will have one hundred Osama Bin Ladens to deal with." **8.** His prediction is now coming true. Al Qaeda has branched out to include not only the brutal ISIS terrorist group, but also autonomous regional organizations such as Khorasan in Syria, Osbat al-Ansar in the Middle East, Abu Sayyaf in The Philippines, Jemmal Islamyic in Indonesia, Silafist Jihadia in North Africa, al Shabaab in Somalia and Boko Harem in Nigeria. Forty-two terrorist organizations from around the world have formally affiliated with ISIS and declared their loyalty to Abu Bakr al-Baghdadi.

The United States announced at the beginning of its air attacks on ISIS that it had disrupted a plan by Khorasan to attack America on American soil. James Clapper, U.S. Director of National Intelligence, said that "in terms of threat to the homeland Khorasan may pose as much of a danger as ISIS". **9.** Pentagon spokesman Lt. Gen. William Mayville said that the Khorasan group was "in the final stages of plans to execute major attacks" before U.S. bombing raids in Syria destroyed their compound and disrupted their plans. **10.**

Yet another al Qaeda affiliate that is now linked with ISIS is Asbat al-Ansar, a terrorist group that exists primarily in Lebanon, and has assassinated Christian religious leaders and bombed night clubs, liquor stores and theaters in that country. Abu Sayyaf has been fighting the government in the Philippines for years, trying to win independence. Their leader Isnilon Hapilon has recently sworn an oath of allegiance to ISIS and its leader al-Baghdadi, and has been kidnapping for ransom in order to raise money for ISIS. Jemmal Islamyic in Indonesia was responsible for the horrific nightclub bombing in Bali that killed 202 and injured 209, and for the lethal bombing at the Marriot Hotel in Jakarta that killed 12 and injured 150. These attacks were done specifically in retaliation for the U.S.-led war on terror, according to a press release by al Qaeda. Silafist Jihadia has attempted over 30 terrorist attacks against different E.U. countries since 2001.

Asbat al-Ansr in Egypt recently announced that it has affiliated with ISIS, and shares the same goals. Its terrorist fighters have been crossing into Libya and supporting attacks on the oil industry there. In retaliation the Egyptian government has been conducting bombing raids into Libya, in an effort to control the incursions of this al Qaeda affiliate. The town of Derna in Libya held a long parade of vehicles recently, displaying the black flag of ISIS and declaring its solidarity with ISIS, thus becoming the first ISIS political center outside the Syrian-Iraqi corridor. The al Qaeda affiliate in Libya beheaded 8 Libyan guards in an attack on the al Ghani oil field, causing Libya to declare that 11 oil fields were non-operational because of Islamic State and al Qaeda attacks. Islamic State militants in Libya have as a goal to completely take over the petroleum industry in war-torn Libya, sell the oil on the black market and use the revenue from that source to finance the ISIS operations in Iraq and Syria. Like Iraq, Libya since American intervention and the murder of Omar Qaddafi has become a divided society prone to violent internal conflict with no discernable path towards stable government. ISIS is now supposedly looking at the port city of Sirte in eastern Libya as its new headquarters if they are routed from Syria. President Barrack Obama has now admitted that American intervention in Libya was his worst mistake as president.

The Somali group al Shabaab, which has affiliated with ISIS, in 2013 attacked Westgate Mall in Nairobi, Kenya, killing 67 shoppers. On November 22, 2014 they crossed into Kenya again, attacked a bus and killed 28 non-Muslims. In another attack by al Shabaab they killed 10 at the presidential palace in Somalia. In their bloodiest terrorist assault to date, on April 2, 2015 they attacked a Christian university in Gerrisa, Kenya, and killed 147 students.

Boko Harem leader Abubaker Shekau of Nigeria made a formal pledge of allegiance to ISIS leader al-Baghdadi, saying in a video, "My brethren…may Allah protect you." Boko Harem is famous for its kidnapping of 200 Nigerian schoolgirls, and for blowing up the Banex Plaza shopping mall, killing 21 and injuring 17. They have announced a formal affiliation with ISIS in a merger that has been called "the alliance from hell". The latest ISIS incursion is into Afghanistan, where they have recently taken over territory previously controlled by the Taliban. They have enforced a strict brand of Islam over the people under their control, and have attracted a number of Taliban supporters to their terrorist group.

Across the Arab world ISIS has become far more dominant, more violent and more threatening than Muslim terrorists ever were before the Bush invasion of Iraq, confirming that Bush did more to activate and accelerate terrorism than he ever did to curtail it. Time magazine`s Karl Vick wrote, in the November 23, 2015 edition:

``ISIS stands as the world`s ultimate terrorist group, operating on levels that no previous extremist organization has ever reached. It exists simultaneously as a military force, a political movement and a terrorist franchise capable of spectacular attacks."

ISIS has in two countries in the past year attempted to seize power through a coup organized by members who had infiltrated top levels of government. On August 2, 2015, the United Arab Emirates arrested 41 ISIS members who had infiltrated and tried to seize control of its government. On October 28, Ethiopia arrested several members of an ISIS cell for the same reason. Muslim countries across the Middle East, and in Africa, have been alerted to ISIS terrorists attempting to infiltrate and seize control of their governments.

Terrorism came home to America once again in December of 2015 when a Muslim couple who were ISIS sympathizers attacked a luncheon in San

Bernardino, California, killing 14 and wounding 22. An ISIS terrorist attack in Paris in November, 2015 resulted in 130 deaths and 368 wounded. On October 31, 2015 ISIS terrorists in Egypt put a bomb on board a Russian passenger plane, blowing it up in mid-air and killing all 224 on board.

The 2003 invasion of Iraq in fact played right into Osama bin Laden's hands. For years, bin Laden had been producing propaganda warning that the US wanted to invade and occupy an oil-rich Middle Eastern country, a prediction that was validated by George Bush with the US invasion of Iraq. The American invasion gave bin Laden increased credibility in the Middle East, and as a result Al-Qaeda and its offshoots, including most particularly ISIS, are having much greater success recruiting new members, not only from countries in the Middle East but also thousands of recruits from England, the USA, Canada and other NATO countries. ISIS leader Abu Bakr al-Baghdadi's call to arms resonated for disaffected Muslims around the world:

"So rush O Muslims and gather around your caliphate, so that you may return as you once were for ages, kings of the earth and knights of war. Come so that you may be honored and esteemed, living as masters with dignity."

The terrorist husband and wife team who did the killing in San Bernardino had been radicalized through training in Saudi Arabia. The husband was an American citizen, born in the USA. Two soldiers killed in separate incidents in Canada were also killed by ISIS sympathizers. According to a report by the Canadian government, over one hundred and sixty Canadians are currently fighting with ISIS in the Middle East. An estimate provided by security intelligence agency Soufan Group suggested that between 27,000 and 31,000 foreign fighters have joined ISIS in the last 18 months. Russia has contributed over 2,400 fighters, third after Saudi Arabia and Tunisia in the number of foreign fighters contributing to the ISIS war effort. A quote from the Soufan Group report stated, "The international response to ISIS is having little effect-Islamic State has energized support from around the world." 11.

In addition to recruiting fighters, ISIS is also attracting young girls from the West who want to marry ISIS fighters. Recently, two 15 year old girls and a 16 year old left their homes in England, made their way to Turkey and crossed the border into Iraq in an attempt to marry ISIS fighters. English government officials have tried desperately to find these girls and return them to England, but to no avail. An Australian supporter of ISIS recently endorsed his 14 year old daughter's marriage to a thirty year old ISIS fighter.

ISIS continually finds newer and more abominable ways to kill the people that it captures, recently caging and then burning alive a Jordanian pilot who had crash landed in ISIS-controlled territory. ISIS has already beheaded a large number of innocent westerners who were in Iraq or Syria as reporters, foreign aid workers or missionaries. One of the primary executioners for ISIS has been identified as a British subject, "Jihadi John", who immigrated to Iraq to fight for the "caliphate". He was later targeted by America's military and was killed in a bombing raid.

A recent report on the internet described ISIS soldiers playing soccer with the head of a decapitated prisoner, extending once again the horror felt by those in the West who have observed on the internet the various deprecations of ISIS soldiers. Few who reacted with abject horror to the desecration of dead bodies by ISIS realize that ISIS soldiers learned this recreational activity of playing soccer with the severed heads of prisoners from American soldiers in Iraq. Joshua Key, an American soldier in Iraq, watched three US soldiers use this tactic in 2003 when they played soccer with the heads of four Iraqi prisoners. The heads had been severed with M-16 machine guns by repeatedly firing at the necks of the Iraqis until their heads were rolling across the ground like soccer balls. The American soldiers then started an impromptu game of soccer, using the Iraqi heads as soccer balls. **12.**

Because of ISIS and its overseas recruitment, Canada and a number of other NATO countries have challenged the basic concepts of freedom, liberty and democracy in their own countries by passing laws that deny human rights that have been painfully acquired over many hundreds of years, going back to the Magna Carta. We saw this happening in the USA after 9/11, when the Department of Homeland Security was formed and laws were passed (The Patriot Act) that allowed the government to spy on private citizens without restraint, jail its citizens without them having recourse to a lawyer, with no charges being filed, and no access to a court of law. One of the sadder stories about anti-terrorism gone bad is the story about Shahawar Matin Siraj, a 21 year old American, who was targeted by the New York anti-terrorism task force, like all anti-terrorist organizations trying to assert its credentials in the fight against terror. Siraj had an IQ of 78, similar to that of a 10 year old. He lived with his parents and spent most of his time at home watching cartoons on television. Informant Osama Eldwoody was paid $100,000 to befriend Siraj at a Muslim drop-in center and lead him into a plot to bomb New York's subway. Before committing to this act of terrorism, Siraj said he would have to ask his Mom if it was okay. Siraj was eventually charged with conspiracy after Eldwoody set him up, and he received a sentence of 30 years in prison. Eldwoody got his $100,000 reward from the government. There are more than a few Americans currently in jail for being guilty of nothing more evil than being gullible, naïve, mentally handicapped and easily manipulated, just like Siraj.

Stephen Harper's Conservative government in Canada passed similar legislation to the Patriot Act in America after two Canadian soldiers were killed by supporters of ISIS. Bitter arguments and demonstrations were provoked across Canada by Bill C-51, a piece of legislation that gives more power to the RCMP and CSIS (Canada's version of the CIA) to track down and arrest potential terrorists. In the process of pursuing terrorists, the Harper government was undermining the very rights and freedoms of Canadian citizens that he claimed to be protecting. In just one example of patriotic zeal gone bad, John Nuttall and his partner Amanda Korody were charged with the terrorist crime of trying to blow up the legislature buildings in Victoria, B.C. They were heroin addicts, living on welfare in a run-down basement apartment, and were easily manipulated by a multi-million dollar RCMP/CSIS sting that involved 200 officers. That "sting" is now being investigated for criminal behavior for leading this naïve and incompetent couple into a "crime" that they could never have organized by themselves. As with the New York Anti-Terrorist Task Force, the Canadian RCMP was using these gullible people as pawns in a twisted and mean-spirited effort to establish their anti-terrorist credentials with their American counterparts. In an ironic twist, Canada is fighting against ISIS in Iraq in order to make Canada safer, yet the only reason ISIS is encouraging attacks in Canada is precisely because Canada is bombing and strafing, killing Muslims in Iraq.

A secret drama is being played out in a Vancouver, BC courtroom today, as five activist groups concerned about the environment are challenging CSIS and the RCMP. Each of these environment protection groups had been actively protesting against a pipeline being built from Alberta's tar sands to the B.C. coast. Documents acquired from the government through Access to

Information legislation indicate that CSIS and the RCMP have been spying on these environment groups, using anti-terrorist legislation as an excuse to illegally interfere with their human rights as guaranteed by Canada's constitution. **13.** CSIS and the RCMP were acting in effect as Prime Minister Harper's personal "secret police", spying on behalf of Harper's friends in the oil industry who helped him get elected, rather than actually protecting Canadians from danger.

Alexis de Tocqueville once said:

"All those who seek to destroy the liberties of a democratic nation ought to know that war is the surest and shortest means to accomplish it."

Also significant, as Canada and other countries are expanding their war with ISIS by conducting bombing raids into Syria, are the words of German philosopher Friedrich Nietzsche, who said:

"Whoever fights monsters should see to it that in the process he does not become a monster…if you gaze long enough into an abyss, the abyss will gaze back into you."

Repeatedly, when terrorist attacks occur in America, France, England or Belgium, politicians, journalists and other celebrities label the attacks as "senseless violence". Yet an exponentially larger number of innocent Muslim civilians have been slaughtered in Iraq and Syria, and had their homes and communities destroyed, because of terrorist attacks by America's menacing military machine, than were ever killed in San Bernardino, Paris, Brussels or New York. Understanding the very real meaning behind the attacks by ISIS terrorists may go a long ways towards resolving the violence and acrimony between Western society and Muslim nations in the Middle East.

At no time since the ill-fated invasion of Iraq have we had a clear, believable explanation from the United States government as to why this outwardly intelligent country would embark on such a blood-thirsty and predatory attack on a virtually defenseless nation. Instead the world watched with increasing skepticism and horror as the Bush regime misled Americans into supporting a war that was neither legal nor necessary. Equally insidious was the manner in which the Bush government fabrications, designed to deceive Americans into supporting this illegal war, were published on the front pages of American newspapers as if they were uncontested fact, thus obliterating the whole concept of investigative journalism. The sycophantic media was obsessed with regurgitating the false and fraudulent claims being peddled by Bush and his neocon supplicants in Washington, claims that were absolutely discredited both before and after the invasion took place. There were no weapons of mass destruction, as guaranteed by Bush and Cheney, absolutely no Iraqi involvement in 9/11, and no connection between al Qaeda and Iraq. Saddam Hussein and Osama bin Laden had very little respect for one another, Osama because he had nothing but disrespect for the way Hussein treated his people and Hussein because he had no interest in harboring a religious fanatic who may upset his tightly-controlled, secular dictatorship. **14.**

Vice President Cheney at one point called Iraq "the geographic base of the terrorists who have had us under assault for many years, but most especially on 9/11". **15.** This was a ludicrous statement to make, given that there was not a shred of evidence connecting Iraq or Saddam Hussein to al Qaeda, to 9/11 or to international terrorism. Another big lie that Cheney repeated on numerous occasions concerned al Qaeda operative and 9/11 hijacker Mohammed Atta meeting with members of the Iraqi intelligence agency. Cheney said, "It's been pretty well confirmed that Atta did go to Prague and he did meet with a senior official of the Iraqi intelligence service." At the same time that Atta was supposed to be in Prague, he was actually traveling from Florida to Virginia Beach, preparing for the 9/11 attacks. The FBI had his rental car contract and his hotel receipts as proof and shared this information with the White House. **16.** Yet Cheney while knowing his statements to be untrue put this comment back into play several times. These bold-faced lies, with absolutely no foundation, were just two of many that Cheney spouted to the obsequious media, knowing that mainstream reporters would acquiesce to his mendacious comments. Media pundits were ignoring the huge demonstrations taking place around the world against the war, including over 500,000 marching in New York against the war, while feverishly regurgitating without any investigation the lies being spouted by Cheney and Bush. Said one astute observer; "The very integrity of journalism was at stake, threatening to make the news completely irrelevant to generations of young Americans".

There is one paradigm that rings true in regard to explaining this predatory invasion, and it involves the cowboy president George Bush and the ever-present cowboy values that permeate American culture. In cowboy movies, the protagonists believe fervently in the adage "doing what needs to be done" and Bush had no issue with asserting his cowboy prerogative and doing what he insisted needed to be done in Iraq.

Before outlining the connection between cowboy values, as replicated in so many cowboy movies, and the invasion of Iraq, it is important to analyze the many lies, distortions, exaggerations and prevarications that the Bush/Cheney regime used to try and justify a war with Iraq. It is only by revealing the lies that we can understand the truth behind the invasion of Iraq.

CHAPTER 2

....

A PENCHANT FOR PREVARICATION

....

"How is the world ruled and led to war? Politicians lie to journalists and then believe the lies when they see them in print."

— KARL KRAUS

Kraus no doubt intended the above comment to be seen as wry humor, but for the Bush White House, it was eerily reflective of actual policy. In his book, <u>A Pretext for War</u>, James Bamford detailed how procedure was followed in the White House leading up to the war.

"First the OSP (Office of Special Plans) supplies false or exaggerated intelligence; then members of the WHIG (White House Iraq Group) leak it to friendly reporters, complete with pre-packaged vivid imagery. Finally when the story breaks, senior Bush officials point to it as proof and parrot the unnamed quotes that they or their colleagues had previously supplied." **1.**

This was the subterfuge used by the Bush administration to push America into war. The deceptions were regurgitated with great enthusiasm by the sycophantic American media and went unchallenged by the toothless Democratic opposition, leading many critics to lament that there was in essence only one political party in America at that time.

Bush began to promote his invasion by attempting to scare Americans with the threat that Iraq possessed fearful weapons of mass destruction. In actual fact, Iraq's army and its military resources had been virtually destroyed in the first Gulf War in 1990-91. The size of its army in 2003 was reduced to 40% of what it had been in 1990, at the beginning of Gulf War 1. Coalition forces sponsored by the United Nations and led by the American military had destroyed Iraqi tanks and most of the rest of Iraq's military hardware in that short-lived and deadly conflict, and on February 12, 1991 a press release issued by the Pentagon said, "Virtually everything military in Iraq is either destroyed or combat ineffective." 2. Iraq had little opportunity to rebuild its military forces in the intervening years because of oppressive sanctions placed on that country by the UN, and by continuous visits by the UN weapons inspection teams throughout the 1990's. Its entire nuclear, biological and chemical collection of weapons was disposed of by the UN teams that visited Iraq during that time. What weapons Iraq had left at its disposal were demolished in the intense, illegal bombing raids conducted by the Brits and the Americans in 1998, and by the 22,000 bombing raids flown by American and British bombers in 2002, hitting 391 "carefully selected targets", all of which were illegal attacks on a sovereign nation. In one particular raid, against Saddam's H-3 airbase in Iraq's western desert, "the US and UK bombers destroyed military communications, eliminated anti-aircraft installations and destroyed a large part of Saddam's air force". 3.

American military intelligence knew of Iraq's inability to defend itself, never mind attack anyone, as did the White House. Before being muzzled by Bush and Cheney, Secretary of State Colin Powell stated in 2001 that economic sanctions against Saddam had worked, and that Saddam "had not developed any significant capability with respect to weapons of mass destruction. He is unable to project conventional power against his neighbors." Condoleezza Rice, Bush's National Security Advisor, echoed Powell's comments, asserting that Iraq had virtually no military presence and was not a threat even to its neighbors in the Middle East, let alone the USA. Rice stated about Saddam Hussein, "We are able to keep weapons from him." 4. Nuclear expert Graham Allison maintained that if a nuclear weapon had been detonated in America prior to the Iraq war, Iraq would not have been on the list of the ten most likely suspects. 5.

Despite the obvious truth concerning Saddam's withering power, Bush continually went on national TV and told the American people of the danger posed by this "menacing" little nation. Bush stated with a great outburst of hyperbole, "This is a fight to save the civilized world", exclaimed, "History has called us into action." and then at the beginning of his illegal assault on Iraq said, "America and coalition forces are in the early stages of military operations to defend the world from grave danger". It was absurd to suggest that Iraq was any kind of threat to the USA, and almost laughable to suggest that this small, militarily-depleted nation represented a danger to the entire world. There has never at any time been any evidence that Saddam Hussein threatened the United States or the world with poisons, diseases, gases, or nuclear weapons. Information suppressed at the time has since made clear that both Tony Blair and George Bush knew well before the invasion that Iraq had no weapons of mass destruction. **6.**

What they also knew was what Hermann Goering said about the Nazi initiatives in starting World War II. Goering said:

"Of course the people don't want war…it is the leaders of the country who determine the policy, and it is always a simple matter to drag the people along, whether it is a democracy, a fascist dictatorship, a parliament or a communist dictatorship. Voice or no voice, the people can always be brought to the bidding of the leaders. That is easy. All you have to do is tell them they are being attacked, and denounce the pacifists for lack of patriotism." **7.**

It worked for the Nazis, and it worked for George Bush.

The determination of the Bush administration to invade Iraq actually began several years before 9/11, and well before Bush was elected president. In 1997, Dick Cheney, the future Vice President, Donald Rumsfeld, the future Secretary of Defense, and Paul Wolfowitz, future Assistant Secretary of Defense, together with a variety of other war hawks who later worked closely with the Bush administration, met in Washington and formed The Project for the New American Century. Although its main goal was world-wide hegemony, a rather esoteric objective, its immediate goal was entirely about the overthrow of Saddam Hussein, and the installation of a puppet government in Iraq that would do the bidding of the White House. The theory behind the plan was that oil was going to become an ever more crucial commodity in the 21st century, and control of oil supplies was crucial to hegemony and world domination. Whoever controls the oil, and more specifically the oil in the Middle East, controls the world. Establishing a strong military base in a Middle Eastern country was paramount to this goal. On January 26, 1998, this group sent a letter to President Bill Clinton asking that he make the removal of Saddam Hussein an objective "vital to our interests in the Gulf." **8.**

In 1999 George Bush was interviewed by the BBC and was asked if the fact that Saddam Hussein was still alive and governing Iraq bothered him at all.

He replied, "It's about time someone finished that job." **9.** No mention was made of weapons of mass destruction, or Iraqi support for terrorism, or of Iraqi connections to al Qaeda. All of this came later, when the Bush regime wanted to sell its phoney war to the American public. There was just an overwhelming desire by these war hawks to invade Iraq and overthrow Saddam Hussein, in order to establish a predominant military base in the Middle East.

In 2001, at the first meeting of the Bush National Security Council, top officials in the Bush cabinet discussed military action against Iraq as a means of getting rid of Saddam Hussein. They appointed a task force on energy headed by Vice President Dick Cheney and the major topic of discussion was "the capture of new and existing oil and gas fields." **10.** Not the capture of dangerous weapons of mass destruction, not to restrain a state sponsor of terrorism, but the capture of oil and gas fields. Paul O'Neill, Bush Secretary of the Treasury, recalled documents produced by the National Security Council titled <u>Plan for Post-Saddam Iraq</u>, which discussed peace-keeping forces and war crimes trials, and another titled <u>Foreign Suitors for Iraqi Oilfield Contracts</u>. In remembering that first NSC meeting, O'Neill said it had a strange feeling of being scripted, and that all of the issues had already been decided, including an attack on Iraq. O'Neill found it disconcerting that the only questions being asked at the meeting were the "how" questions, and yet it was the "why" questions that were most intrinsic to the issue. Said O'Neill, "Who exactly was pushing this foreign policy? Why Saddam, why now and why was this central to U.S. interests?" None of those questions were being asked, discussed or answered. **11.**

Vice President Dick Cheney, while still CEO at Halliburton, gave an address to the London Petroleum Institute in 1999 in which he stated, "By 2010 we will need on the order of an additional fifty million barrels of oil a day. So where is the oil going to come from? While many of the regions of the world offer great oil opportunities, the Middle East, with two thirds of the world's oil and the lowest cost, is still where the prize ultimately lies." **12.** Even before 9/11 there was a veritable parade of oil industry executives making their way to Cheney's office when he became Vice President, for secret meetings to discuss this "prize". From these secret meetings came maps of the oil fields of Iraq. **13.** In discussing the reasons for attacking Iraq, rather than Iran or North Korea, the other two members of Bush's infamous "Axis of Evil", war hawk Paul Wolfowitz also addressed the topic of oil when he said, "We had virtually no economic options with Iraq. The country floats on a sea of oil." **14.**

The day after the 9/11 attacks, Bush met with his cabinet and the entire focus of that meeting was to establish a link between Saddam and Al Qaeda, in order to justify an invasion of Iraq. Counter-terrorism Coordinator Richard Clarke, who had worked for various administrations in Washington for 30 years, went to the White House for a series of meetings that he thought would focus on Al Qaeda.

"I expected to go back to a round of meetings examining what the next attacks could be, what our vulnerabilities were, what we could do about them in the short term. Instead I walked into a series of discussions about Iraq. At first I was incredulous that we were talking about something other than getting Al Qaeda. Then I realized with almost a sharp pain that Rumsfeld and Wolfowitz were going to try and take advantage of this national tragedy to promote their agenda about Iraq. Since the beginning of the administration, they had been pressing for a war in Iraq. Later in the day, Secretary Rumsfeld complained that there were no decent targets for bombing in Afghanistan and that we should consider bombing Iraq which, he said, had better targets. At first I thought Rumsfeld was joking, but he was serious." **15.**

Clarke said he became so frustrated with the Rumsfeld/Wolfowitz obsession with Iraq, he blurted out:

"Having been attacked by al Qaeda, for us now to go bombing Iraq in response would be like invading Mexico after the Japanese attacked us at Pearl Harbor." **16.**

Clarke's perceptive analogy and its implications were ignored as the neocon war hawks continued with their obsession to invade Iraq. Rumsfeld, Cheney and Wolfowitz had hijacked that crucial meeting and moved the focus from the real terrorists, al Qaeda, to oil-rich Iraq. Clarke wrote that at that same meeting President Bush pulled him and a couple of his aides aside and "testily" asked him to try to find evidence that Saddam Hussein was connected to the 9/11 terrorist attacks. **17.** Several days later Clarke wrote a report stating that there was no evidence of Iraqi involvement in 9/11 and got it signed by all relevant agencies, including the FBI and the CIA. At a later meeting of Deputy Secretaries chaired by Steve Hadley, Deputy Secretary of Defense Paul Wolfowitz responded to Clarke's report by saying, "Well, I just don't understand why we are beginning by talking about this one man bin Laden." Clarke replied that he was talking about Osama bin Laden and his al Qaeda network because he posed "an immediate and serious threat to the United States." According to Clarke, Wolfowitz turned to him and said, "You give bin Laden too much credit. He could not do all these things like the 1993 attack on New York, not without a state sponsor. Just because the FBI and CIA have failed to find the linkages does not mean they don't exist." **18.** The White House senior staff then rejected Clarke's report and sent it back to be re-written, the standard procedure any time that information contradicted the Bush regime's obsession with invading Iraq.

Repeated attempts by Bush to connect Saddam to 9/11 were fruitless, because Al Qaeda had no connection to Saddam Hussein before the invasion. Clarke felt that the invasion of Iraq greatly hampered the war on terror, and was a distraction from the real terrorists. Clarke claimed in his book <u>Against All Enemies</u> that this conclusion was understood by the intelligence community at the time of 9/11. But top Bush administration officials were pre-occupied with finding a link between Iraq and 9/11 and thus, Clarke argued, the Iraq war distracted attention and resources from the war in Afghanistan and the hunt for Osama bin Laden. Clarke's account of the post-9/11 period was supported in later years by Marine Lieutenant General Greg Newbold, former director of operations for the Joint Chiefs of Staff, and by Army General John Batiste, former commander of the First Infantry Division. Consistent with Clarke's account of the period, Newbold told an interviewer in 2007 of his dismay over the focus on Iraq, which seemed "irrelevant". He stated that "Saddam Hussein, and not Osama bin Laden or Mullah Omar, was most on the Bush administration's mind." Batiste, who would go on to have a primary role in the war in Iraq, saw the Iraq war plan develop "even before 9/11" and "solidify" thereafter.

At a press conference on August 21, 2006 Bush was asked what evidence he had before the invasion that Iraq was involved in the 9/11 attacks. He replied by saying "nothing." He was asked the same question in February of 2007 and again replied by saying "nothing". **19.** The 9/11 Commission Report confirmed that judgement when it stated that there was absolutely no connection between Iraq and 9/11. Yet rhetoric by administration members before the invasion was consistently laden with strident declarations about Saddam and his linkage to 9/11. These fabricated prevarications were but a façade, a web of bold-faced lies fed to the American public to create a foundation upon which to launch this illegal and highly predatory war. Even when Bush and other regime members reluctantly admitted that there was no connection between Saddam and al Qaeda, or between Saddam and 9/11, the arrogant Cheney was still grumbling about illusive connections that had not yet been discovered.

On September 17, 2001 Bush signed a Top Secret order that both laid out his plan for the war in Afghanistan and directed the Pentagon to begin military planning for an invasion of Iraq. **20.** In order to sell the Iraq war to the American public, a secretive committee called the Policy Counterterrorism Evaluation Group was formed. David Wurmser, who chaired this shadowy committee, was a protégé of Bush insider and war hawk Richard Perle, informally known as "The Prince of Darkness". Wurmser had a long history of promoting pro-Israeli propaganda that included plans for a military attack on Iraq. The primary purpose of the unit was to counter the CIA, whose analysis quite honestly showed no connection between Saddam and 9/11, and downplayed the threat of weapons of mass destruction. The CIA's analysis, said Perle, "isn't worth the paper it is printed on." **21.** As with the other war hawks, Perle had little use for any assessment that didn't support his obsession with invading Iraq. Perle was of course wrong, but as with Wolfowitz and the rest of the war hawks in Bush's White House, being wrong did not prevent the avalanche of lies that laid the foundation for the vicious, bloodthirsty attack on the Iraqi people.

In commenting about the work of Wurmser's group, author David Bamford in his book A Pretext for War stated:

"Instead of an honest, unbiased review of intelligence such as the CIA was charged with producing, the Wurmser intelligence unit would pluck selective bits and pieces of thread from a giant ball of yarn and weave them together into a frightening tapestry." 22.

Retired Air Force Lt. Col. Karen Kwiatkowski agreed with Bamford's assessment and said of Wurmser's secretive group:

"It wasn't intelligence. It was propaganda. They'd take a little bit of intelligence, cherry-pick it, make it sound much more exciting, usually by taking it out of context, often by juxtaposition of two pieces of information that don't belong together." 23.

At the same time that Wurmser's group was manipulating intelligence to fit the pre-ordained "invasion of Iraq" theme, a very secretive, cloak-and-dagger media company called The Rendon Group was hired by the Bush regime and given a contract of $100,000 a month to produce anti-Saddam propaganda worldwide. In total, the Rendon Group was paid over $200,000,000 by the CIA and Pentagon, all taxpayer dollars, to character-assassinate Saddam and pave the way to an invasion. 24.

Scott Ritter, former arms inspector in Iraq, commented:

"I think what you're seeing is the need of the United States government to turn to commercial enterprises like The Rendon Group to do the kind of lying and distortion of truth in terms of peddling disinformation to the media that the government can't do for itself." 25.

The secretive Wurmser committee was later rolled into a new group called the Office of Special Plans (OSP), and Wurmser joined Cheney's staff. Lt. Col. Kwiatkowski had this to say about OSP:

"The public heard what they were supposed to hear, what the OSP wanted them to hear. They spent their energy gathering pieces of information and creating a propaganda story line, which is the same story line we heard the President and Vice President Cheney tell the American people in the fall of 2002. The very phrases they used are coming back to haunt them because they are blatantly false and not based on any intelligence. The OSP and the Vice President's office were critical in this propaganda effort-to convince Americans that there was some just requirement for pre-emptive war. The Congress was misled, it was lied to. At a very minimum, that is a subversion of the Constitution. A pre-emptive war based on what we knew was not a pressing need is not what this country stands for." **26.**

The "faulty intelligence" that Bush blamed for his decision to invade Iraq was never faulty, but instead was deliberately manipulated to fit the scenario for an invasion. A U.S. government source in Washington with 20 years of experience in intelligence stated; "This administration is capable of any lie in order to advance its war goal in Iraq." **27.**

Two international relations scholars added that "the President's claim about Iraqi threats should be viewed as transparent attempts to scare Americans into supporting a war." **28.**

Critics of the Bush regime were reluctant to publically condemn the march to war because of the well-established record of the Bush regime for revenge and retribution, punishing those who didn't have the requisite loyalty while rewarding those who supported the stream of lies emanating from the Bush White House. One need look no further than the "outing" of one of its own, Valerie Plame, a CIA operative whose clandestine role was made public by Scooter Libby. Vice President Dick Cheney, Libby's immediate supervisor, no doubt directed Libby to exact revenge on Plame's husband, Joe Wilson, for not supporting Bush's outrageous lie about uranium from Niger. Revealing Plame's true identity as a CIA operative, something even her best friends didn't know, was a serious violation of the law, because it exposed and compromised both her and all of her clandestine contacts around the world. Cheney was able to circumvent his insidious role in the affair by passing the blame on to Libby, the fall guy, who was convicted but then pardoned by Bush. Cheney's cowardice in not owning up to his actions was not something new; like George Bush, Cheney had also dodged the draft for Vietnam, passing up his turn to serve but having no problem with playing the role of the 'war hero' when it was other young Americans being sent to die. The purging of Paul O'Neill, Brent Scowcroft and Colin Powell from this administration, together with the "outing" of Valerie Plame, left little to the imagination in regard to the vindictive nature of the Bush/Cheney regime. George Tenet, director of the CIA at the time of the invasion of Iraq, played the game far more effectively than O'Neill, Joe Wilson, Scowcroft or Colin Powell, taking the heat away from the Bush regime by accepting blame that the CIA didn't deserve for the Bush/

Cheney lies about Iraq. He resigned in 2004 and on December 14 of that year was given his just reward for taking Bush and Cheney off the hook by lying about CIA culpability. He was awarded the Presidential Medal of Freedom. Many astute observers were astounded that such an unworthy candidate would receive the highest award given in the United States to a civilian, but George Bush knew how to reward his friends, and punish his enemies.

In one of his many lies about Saddam's nuclear capability, Bush ignored the advice of the CIA in regard to falsified information from IAEA. On September 7, 2002 Bush told reporters gathered at Camp David about "alarming" new evidence. He said:

"A report came out of the <u>International Atomic Energy Agency</u> that the Iraqis were six months away from developing a weapon. I don't know what more evidence we need."

A week later Bush repeated his nuclear charge by again invoking the IAEA report on his weekly radio address:

"Saddam Hussein has the scientists and infrastructure for a nuclear weapons program and has illicitly sought to purchase the equipment needed to enrich uranium for a nuclear weapon."

Bush was deliberately lying to the American people, a practice with which he was quite adept. He was well aware, because he had been told by the CIA, that the IAEA document he was referring to was from 1996, and it described a weapons program that UN inspectors had long ago dismantled. This did not prevent Bush from presenting this stale-dated information as if it were current. **29.**

That Bush would openly deceive the American people in order to promote his predatory war was not an aberration, for his facility in distorting the truth was well-documented. When the twin towers went down in the 9/11 terrorist attack Bush was at an elementary school in Florida. When asked on December 4, 2001 about when he first learned of the attacks he said, "I was sitting outside the classroom waiting to go in and I saw an airplane hit the tower-the TV was obviously on, and I used to fly myself and I said 'There's one terrible pilot' and I said 'It must have been a horrible accident'". He repeated that same story a month later, on January 5, 2002, to an audience in California.

But this story could not possibly have been true because there was no video available to the TV networks of the first plane hitting the Twin Towers until late in the evening of 9/11, many hours after Bush had left that school and had flown away on Air Force One. This falsehood followed his previous deceptions about his experience as a pilot with the Texas National Guard, and his lies about trying to sign up for the Vietnam War and being rejected. In fact, he had previously bragged to his friends about how he had dodged the draft for Vietnam, and never had any intention of signing up for the military. Bush previously stated he had worked to pass legislation while Governor of Texas for a Patients' Bill of Rights. In fact he had vetoed that legislation, only to have his veto overturned. Bush also lied about his conversion to Christianity, a bizarrely contradictory topic upon which to be playing fast and loose with the truth. On several occasions Bush told a story about going for a walk with the famous Christian Billy Graham while Graham was visiting the Bush family retreat at Walker's Point. During their make-believe conversation about accepting Jesus as his personal savior, Graham supposedly had a profound influence on Bush, and following that interaction, Bush was convinced that he should become a born-again Christian. When asked about this, Graham denied ever going for a walk with George W. Bush and said he had never discussed religious beliefs with the younger Bush. He was shocked that Bush gave him credit for his conversion, and said he played no part whatsoever in Bush's decision to become a born-again Christian. It was later revealed that a little-known televangelist from Texas, Arthur Blessitt, actually was responsible for Bush's conversion. Blessit became famous for carrying a cross, similar to the cross Jesus was nailed to, around the world to bring world-wide attention to Christianity. This falsified revelation of how Bush became a born-again Christian came as no surprise to Eric Alterman, whose article "Liar, Liar", published in Nation on December 11, 2006 revealed the web of deceit perpetrated by Bush leading up to the invasion of Iraq. Among his other serious deceptions, Bush stated publicly that Saddam Hussein would not allow weapons inspectors to do their job, when in fact UN weapons inspectors were in Iraq and doing excellent work on behalf of the United Nations, when they got ordered out by Bush, so that he could start his war. Later, just before the 2004 election, Bush stated that Secretary of Defence Rumsfeld would stay in his job "come hell or high water", when in fact Bush had already made plans to replace Rumsfeld with Robert Gates. Bush admitted that lie after the election, stating in effect that he lied because he could. A poll in April, 2005 showed that the majority of

Americans believed Bush "deliberately misled the American public" in the lead-up to war with Iraq.

Colin Brown and Andy McSmith in The Independent wrote an article titled Diplomat's Suppressed Document Lays Bare the Lies Behind Iraq War. Published on December 15, 2006, this article quoted key British negotiator at the UN Carne Ross as saying:

"There was no intelligence evidence of significant holdings of chemical weapons, biological weapons or nuclear material held by the Iraqi dictator before the invasion. Moreover, there was no intelligence or assessment during my time on the job that Iraq had any intention to launch an attack against its neighbors or the UK or the US".

Carl Cannon in his article Untruth and Consequence, published in Atlantic in January, 2007 revealed that while in Virginia Bush met with House Speaker Bob Kiss and they began talking about raising twins. Bush said, "I've been to war and I've raised twins. If I had a choice I would choose to go to war." Good joke, but it was based on a lie. Bush has never been to war. He had a chance, during the Vietnam War, but he had his Dad get him a position in the Texas National Guard so that he could dodge the draft.

In May of 2003 George Bush stated publicly "We have found the weapons of mass destruction." No WMD capability was ever found in Iraq. On the U.S.S Lincoln he announced, "Major combat operations in Iraq have ended". In fact, they had not ended. Thirteen years later Iraq is still consumed by civil war, and the American military is still enmeshed in a conflict that seemingly has no end.

In regard to Bush's relationship to the truth, British Middle East scholar Toby Dodge said:

"The documents show that the case for weapons of mass destruction was based on thin intelligence and was used to inflate the evidence to the level of mendacity." **30.**

The CIA had one of its greatest successes during this time when Iraqi Foreign Minister Naji Sabri was "turned" and agreed to provide the CIA with top-secret information from inside Saddam Hussein's government. He told the CIA that Iraq had no Weapons of Mass Destruction programs. George Tenet met with Bush on Sept. 18, 2002 and shared this information with him. "The president had no interest in this information", said one CIA officer. Said another, "Bush didn't give a fuck about the intelligence. He had his mind made up." **31.**

National security and intelligence analyst John Prados also addressed the topic of Bush mendacity. He said in his book <u>Hoodwinked</u> that the Bush "scheme to convince America and the world that war with Iraq was necessary and urgent was a case study in government dishonesty that required patently untrue public statements and egregious manipulation of intelligence". **32.**

In February of 2002, detailed planning for an invasion of Iraq began, and that planning was completed and in place by early summer of 2002, well before Bush went to Congress to get approval for an invasion.

In October of 2002, VP Cheney met with major US oil companies, including Halliburton, the corporation for which he had been CEO and the company that profited most from the Iraqi war. Cheney continued to collect a salary of almost $200,000 a year from Halliburton, and continued to hold over $10 million in Halliburton shares, while taking a leading role in planning a war in which Halliburton earned a profit of over $50 billion. Halliburton re-paid Cheney and Bush when the defense contractor funneled over $500,000 to the Republican Party to help get Bush/Cheney re-elected in 2004. **33.** Cheney was defining with clarity the whole concept of conflict of interest, behaving openly and defiantly like a 3rd world dictator, as he stole the lives of America's young soldiers while cashing in personally on America's bloated military budget.

At the same time that Cheney was arranging for his lucrative Halliburton pension plan, Phillip Carroll, ex-CEO of Shell Oil, was being hired by the Pentagon to draft a strategy paper for developing Iraq's oil sector. He was subsequently given a position by George Bush on the <u>Policy Planning Advisory Board</u> of the Iraqi oil ministry. A subsidiary of Halliburton was contracted to draw up plans to extinguish oil well fires that resulted from a war with Iraq, well before Bush went to Congress with his proposal for military action. **34.**

There was more than one voice of caution arguing against the ill-fated assault on Iraq in the months leading up to the invasion. Retired Air Force General Brent Scowcroft on August 4, 2002 warned on morning television against an invasion of Iraq. Scowcroft chaired the President's <u>Foreign Intelligence Board</u>

and was considered to be a national security expert. He warned that an invasion "could turn the whole region into a cauldron and thus destroy the war on terrorism." **35.** In an article titled <u>Sins of the Son</u> in the Washington Post, January 20, 2008, Michael Getler stated that this warning from Scowcroft came indirectly from George H. W. Bush, a very close friend of Scowcroft. Getler suggested that Bush Sr. used Scowcroft as a surrogate- "A worried father's only way of communicating with his bellicose son". **36.** The White House reacted to Scowcroft's concerns by ignoring his warning, and by increasing the intensity of the confidence game being played on the American people. Scowcroft was denied access to the White House and eventually purged from the White House staff, yet another revenge response by a regime that was ruthless in castigating anyone on staff who did not give 100% support to the invasion of Iraq. George W. Bush's conservative biographers, Peter and Rachel Schweitzer, quoted him as saying at the time, in reference to his father's good friend, "Scowcroft has become a pain in the ass in his old age." **37.**

Little-known Illinois Senator Barrack Obama supported Scowcroft's warning in 2002 when he said:

"War with Iraq would require U.S. occupation of undetermined length, at undetermined cost, with undetermined consequences. An invasion of Iraq without a clear rationale and without strong international support will only fan the flames of the Middle East and encourage the worst rather than the best impulses of the Arab world, while strengthening the recruitment arm of al Qaeda." **38.**

The many hypocritical statements of the Bush regime knew no limitation as Bush and Cheney marched the USA inexorably to war. Despite this background of preparation for war with oil being the number one talking point, Bush could still repeatedly tell the American people that weapons of mass destruction and Saddam's connection to 9/11 and al Qaeda were the rationale for war. As late as March of 2003, at a time when the CIA and the White House were well aware that weapons of mass destruction did not exist in Iraq, Bush stated in a press conference that weapons of mass destruction was the "signal question" that justified the invasion of Iraq.

Bush, Cheney and Condoleezza Rice made the ominous threat on television that "we don't want the smoking gun to be a mushroom cloud", at a time when they knew that Iraq had no nuclear weapons capability. **39.** This phrase was actually concocted by the White House public relations department, and was meant to convey that Iraq had already committed a crime (the smoking gun analogy) and that Iraq already had nuclear weapons and was prepared to use them in an assault that would be even worse than 9/11. This second metaphor was an outright lie, for UN weapons inspectors had already disabled Saddam's nuclear capability in the 1990's and this was verified by the CIA. In November 2002, the UN and IAEA inspectors were readmitted to Iraq and found no evidence of a nuclear weapons program. On March 7, 2003, IAEA chief Mohammed El Baradei announced that after 3 months of "intrusive" inspections, there was no evidence of Saddam reviving his nuclear weapons program. **40.** On February 8, 2004, Dr. Hans Blix, in an interview on BBC TV, accused the U.S. and UK governments of dramatizing the threat of weapons of mass destruction in Iraq, in order to strengthen the case for the 2003 war against the government of Saddam Hussein. So much of the rationale set forth by the Bush regime to validate war seemed to emanate from a public relations point of view, designed to create a false impression with the American public, in effect a massive con job, rather than from an honest assessment of the military and political realities existing between America and Iraq.

In 2002, Scott Ritter, a former UNSCOM weapons inspector for 8 years and for 12 years a Marine intelligence officer, heavily criticized the Bush administration and media outlets for using the testimony of former Iraqi kick-back specialist Khidir Hamza, who defected from Iraq in 1994, as a rationale for invading Iraq

Ritter exclaimed;

"We seized the entire records of the Iraqi nuclear program, especially the administrative records. We got the names of everybody, where they worked, what they did, and the top of the list, Saddam's "bombmaker", was a man named Jafar Dhia Jafar, not Khidir Hamza, and if you go down the list of the senior administrative personnel you will not find Hamza's name in there. In fact, we didn't find his name at all. Because in 1990, he didn't work for the Iraqi nuclear program. He had no knowledge of it because he worked as a kickback specialist for Hussein Kamel in the Presidential Palace. He goes into northern Iraq and meets up with Ahmad Chalabi. He walks in and says, I'm Saddam's 'bombmaker'. So they call the CIA and they (the CIA) say, 'We know who you are, you're not Saddam's 'bombmaker', go sell your story to someone else.' And he was released, he was rejected by all intelligence services at the time, he's a fraud. And here we are, someone who the CIA knows is a fraud, the US Government knows is a fraud, is allowed to sit in front of the United States Senate Committee on Foreign Relations and give testimony as an expert witness. I got a problem with that, I got a problem with the American media, and I've told them over and over and over again that this man is a documentable fraud, a fake, and yet they allow him to go on CNN, MSNBC, CNBC and testify as if he actually knows what he is talking about." **41.**

Hamza's lies to that committee were used as part of the rationale for America's invasion. Most sinister is the fact that everyone in the White House, including George Bush and Dick Cheney, knew he was lying and yet they supported his testimony without qualification.

Scott Ritter had produced in the year 2000 a documentary titled "Shifting Sands", and in that documentary he referred to Iraq as a "defanged tiger". He itemized how UN inspectors had successfully eliminated "significant Iraqi Weapons of Mass Destruction capabilities". **42.** Yet the White House ignored this first-hand information, and continued to exaggerate the threat Iraq posed to the United States, and to the world.

In a State of the Union address to Congress in early 2003, in attempting to convince legislators of the need for war, George Bush stated, "The British government has learned that Saddam Hussein recently sought significant quantities of uranium from Niger". This information came from a fraudulent set of documents from Italy. The CIA had determined four months previously that of the two uranium mines referred to in the documents, one was flooded and the other was under the control of the French. Niger had stringent controls placed on the shipment of uranium by the International Atomic Energy Agency, and could never have shipped uranium to Iraq without the consent of the IAEA. **43.** The CIA further was aware that Saddam had enough uranium for any purpose and didn't need the fictional uranium from Niger. The actual documents from which this information had been drawn were obviously forged, with flaws in the letterhead, forged signatures, misspelled words and incorrect titles for individuals. One letter in those documents was forged so incompetently that the dates on the letter had it being delivered two weeks before it was written. In December of 2001, Greg Theilman, director of strategic proliferation and military affairs at the State Department, told Colin

Powell "A whole lot of things told us that the report was bogus. This wasn't highly contested. There weren't strong advocates on the other side. It was done, shot down". On November 20, 2001 the U.S. embassy in Niamey, the capital city of Niger, had issued a report stating that there was no possibility that the government of Niger had directed any yellowcake uranium to Iraq. **44.** Both the ambassador to Niger and the former ambassador Joe Wilson investigated these claims and vehemently denied that there was any connection between Iraq and Niger, in regard to yellowcake uranium. The CIA passed this information on to George Bush in October of 2002, warning him not to use the uranium report in a speech. Bush ignored this advice and used this information in an address to Congress four months later, openly lying about this fictitious uranium because he knew that if he was called out on this deception, he could blame the British, or his own CIA. Lying to Congress is a violation of the Constitution. Predictably, the mainstream media in the U.S. gave Bush another free pass, accepting this fabrication and presenting it to the public as if it was proven fact, at a time when there was overwhelming evidence that what Bush stated in his address to Congress was a lie. Bush and Cheney continually insulted the Constitution of the United States, criminally deceiving the American people

Condoleezza Rice emulated her boss when it came to misleading comments about the fictitious uranium by insisting three times that the White House had no knowledge about the doubts surrounding the uranium story. She said, "If there were any doubts about the underlying intelligence to that National Intelligence Estimate, those doubts were not communicated to the President, to the Vice President or to me." Condoleezza Rice had been sent an explicit CIA memorandum expressing doubts regarding the presence of uranium claims in Bush's October Cincinnati speech. **45.** She said this at a time when she had access to Theilman's report, the report from the U.S. embassy in Niger, and the first-person report by Joe Wilson.

This was not the only time that Rice lied to the American public. At the 9/11 Commission of Inquiry Rice was equally deceptive, stating, "I don't think anyone could have predicted that these people would try to use a plane as a missile." Perhaps the average person on the street could not have predicted that, but the President's National Security Advisor should have been aware of the well-documented history of the threat of planes being used as missiles to attack public buildings. In a highly-publicized incident in France in1994

French commandos killed a group of Algerian terrorists who had planned to hijack a commercial aircraft and crash it into the Eiffel Tower. In 1995 terrorist Abdul Hakim Murad revealed a terrorist plot to hijack a commercial aircraft and fly it into CIA headquarters. In 1999 a report prepared by the National Intelligence Council warned that terrorists might hijack a plane and fly it into government targets. In October 2000 the government staged mock rescue exercises responding to a scenario in which a hijacked plane was flown into the Pentagon. In early 2001 reports emanating from Jordan, Russia, Germany, Italy and Egypt all warned of plans by Middle Eastern terrorists to hijack commercial aircraft and crash them into symbols of American culture. The Washington Post revealed that one month before the 9/11 attacks President Bush and his top advisors, including Rice, had been informed by the CIA that terrorists associated with Osama bin Laden planned to hijack planes and crash them into prominent buildings. With these and so many more incidents in which plans to crash commercial aircraft into prominent landmarks were revealed, it is truly astounding that Rice would find this tactic impossible to predict. **46.** Rice was either blatantly lying or incredibly incompetent at her job, given that knowing this information was an integral part of her work assignment as National Security Advisor. Compounding her lack of integrity, Rice responded to a question from Fox News about links between Saddam Hussein and Osama bin Laden by stating, ""'Iraq clearly has links to terrorism…links to terrorism that would include al Qaeda". **47.** She stated this despite having no evidence of a link between Saddam and Osama, and no evidence of Iraq being a state sponsor of terrorism. Rice and the other Bush regime members constantly made comments that were far removed from the truth, both before and after the invasion of Iraq, assuming that the patriotic fervor of the press would subvert the whole concept of journalistic integrity.

Knight-Ridder reporters Warren Strobel and Jonathon Landay found a number of senior U.S. officials with access to intelligence on Iraq who thought claims by the Bush regime were fraudulent.

"While President Bush marshals congressional and international support for invading Iraq, a growing number of military officers, intelligence professionals and diplomats in his own government privately have deep misgivings about the administration's double-time march toward war. Administration hawks have exaggerated evidence of the threat that Iraqi leader Saddam Hussein possesses, including distorting his links to the al Qaeda terrorist network. They charge that the administration squelches dissenting views and that intelligence analysts are under intense pressure to produce reports supporting the White House's argument that Saddam poses such an immediate threat to the United States that pre-emptive military action is necessary." **48.**

Colin Powell, representing the Bush regime, went to the U.N. on February 5, 2003 and talked about the UAV (unmanned aerial vehicles) threat as a key justification for going to war. Powell stated, "Iraq could use these small UAV's, which have a wingspan of only a few meters, to deliver biological agents to its neighbors or, if transported, to other countries, including the United States." **49.** Dick Cheney repeated this fabrication in detail to Congress. The intelligence behind this statement was of course fraudulent. The drones were made for observation, not delivery of chemical or biological agents. Florida senator Bill Nelson was one of the many members of Congress to vote in favor of war with Iraq in large part because of the evidence about these drones. He said, "The degree of specificity I was given a year and a half ago, prior to my vote, was not only inaccurate, it was patently false." **50.** When asked about the drone scenario, Air Force Major General Robert Boyd stated that the unmanned vehicles were intended for overhead reconnaissance, and were too small for weapons delivery. **51.**

Other Bush administration distortions of the truth included the stories about mobile weapons labs, and the fabrication that al-Qaeda operative and hijacker Mohamed Atta had met with Iraqi security people in Prague. **52.** As was their penchant throughout the lead-up to the invasion, the American media gave Bush a free pass, allowing him to blatantly lie to the entire country knowing that investigative journalism had sold out to a twisted version of journalistic patriotism.

On May 29, 2003, Andrew Gilligan appeared on the BBC's Today program. Among the contentions he made in his report were that the government "ordered the September dossier (a British Government dossier on WMD) to be sexed up, to be made more exciting, and ordered more facts to be...discovered." He concluded that "the intelligence and facts were being fixed around the policy." That policy was to invade Iraq.

This dossier was not the only fraudulent British government document. At his infamous address at the U.N., Colin Powell stated, "Every statement I make today is backed up by sources, solid sources." One of his solid sources was a nineteen page dossier entitled <u>Iraq: Its Infrastructure of Concealment, Deception and Intimidation</u>, produced by the British government. This document had in fact been plagiarized from a report written by Ibrahim al-Marashi. It was plagiarized so badly by the British it even included al-Marashi's many grammatical and typographical mistakes. In particular pages 6-16 of al-Marashi's report were copied directly into the British dossier, word for word. Most outrageous is that al-Marashi's report was written twelve years previously, and despite being fully aware of that, Powell presented the British dossier as being current information. **53.** This "spectacular" performance by Colin Powell, forced on him by George Bush and Dick Cheney, was later described by Powell as the absolute low point of his political career. Virtually every claim he made at the UN was contradicted by the intelligence community and by UN inspectors. Colin Powell was later marginalized, criticized and eventually dismissed as Secretary of State for not having the requisite enthusiasm for war, and for wanting to be more honest with the American people. He was not the only one. Anyone in the White House who expressed reservations about Bush's war plans was summarily dismissed or forced to resign, in the same way that any information that didn't fit the Bush script was discarded.

In the buildup to the 2003 war, the <u>New York Times</u> published a number of stories claiming to prove that Iraq possessed WMD. One story in particular, written by reporter Judith Miller, helped persuade the American public that Iraq had WMD. In September 2002 she wrote about an intercepted shipment of aluminum tubes which the <u>New York Times</u> said were to be used to develop nuclear material. **54.** It is now generally understood that they were not intended or well suited for that purpose at all but rather were designed for artillery rockets.

In his book <u>Hoodwinked</u>, John Prados stated:

"Aluminum had not been used for centrifuges since the 1950's. The dimensions of the Iraqi tubes were wrong as well. In late 2001 physicist Houston G. Wood III was asked to review the evidence and concluded that the doubts were well-founded." **55.**

Director General ElBaradei of the International Atomic Energy Agency announced on March 7, 2003 that:

"Iraq's efforts to import these aluminum tubes were not likely to have been related to the manufacture of centrifuges and it was highly unlikely that Iraq could have achieved the considerable redesign needed to use them in a revived centrifuge program." 56.

British intelligence also stated that they believed the tubes were not for nuclear programs. Dick Cheney, with absolutely no evidence to support his argument, nevertheless stated "I think Mr. ElBaradei frankly is wrong." Six months later, after Cheney was proven to be wrong, he was asked about his claim and responded by saying he had "misspoken". 57. What he should have said but didn't have the courage to say is that he had deliberately lied to the American people in an effort to sell them his illegal, predatory war, a war that earned Mr. Cheney a handsome profit on his millions of dollars in Halliburton shares. Repeatedly lying, and making a huge profit from the war he started, are not the only unethical behaviors demonstrated by the recalcitrant Vice President. He personally went to CIA headquarters on a number of occasions to try and coerce intelligence that would suggest that Iraq had a highly-developed and dangerous accumulation of weapons of mass destruction, an unprecedented and extremely unethical behavior for any vice president. Vince Cannistraro, former head of counterintelligence for the CIA said, "Basically 'cooked' information is working its way into high-level pronouncements and there's a lot of unhappiness about it in intelligence, especially among analysts at the CIA". One senior CIA official said "the hammering of analysts was greater than any he had seen in 32 years at the CIA". 58.

Despite solid evidence that the tubes referenced by Cheney and Bush had nothing to do with weapons of mass destruction, the story in the New York Times was followed up with television appearances by Colin Powell, Donald Rumsfeld and Condoleezza Rice, all pointing to the story as part of the basis for taking military action against Iraq. All three were blatantly lying to the American people as they tried to sell an illegal war to America, for the information was already available that strongly refuted that the tubes were for centrifuges.

Judith Miller's sources were introduced to her by Ahmed Chalabi, an Iraqi exile and convicted embezzler favorable to a U.S. invasion of Iraq because he hoped to succeed Saddam as Iraq's leader. In the 1980's Chalabi had founded the Petra Bank in Jordan, but was forced to flee that country for England in

1989 amidst charges of embezzlement, forgery, theft, and currency speculation. He was convicted of these charges "in absentia" and was sentenced to 22
years of hard labor and a $230 million fine. Chalabi, like Hamza, on several
occasions created fictional stories about Saddam's so-called weapons of mass
destruction programs in order to gain credibility with the White House. Each
time his claims were proven to be false by weapons inspectors he would say,
"Oh, Saddam's just too smart for you. He moved them." Weapons inspector
Scott Ritter, cynical of Chalabi's claims, reacted by asking, "How do you move
an underground facility?"

Chalabi was in 2004 identified by the CIA as a spy for the Iranian government, and was selling top-secret information to Iran. His close friendships
with neocons Paul Wolfowitz, Douglas Feith, Andrew Card and Ricard Perle
left little doubt as to the source of this top secret information. Chalabi had
no credibility outside the White House, for it soon became apparent that
he was selling fantasy stories in a vain attempt to try and succeed Saddam
as Iraq's leader. A top official in the Clinton administration dismissed him by
saying, "He represents four or five guys in London who wear nice suits and
have a fax machine." Despite his total lack of integrity, his fantasy stories to
the Bush regime eventually earned Chalabi and his Iraqi National Congress
$200,000,000 in American taxpayer dollars, paid out by the Pentagon and the
CIA in support of his lies about Saddam's illusive weapons programs. Chalabi
prospered in large part because of the support he received from Judith Miller
in The New York Times, and the support he received from all the neocon war
hawks close to the power elite in the White House. **59.**

Miller repeatedly used Chalabi and a number of other discredited Iraqi exiles
as her sources. Miller was listed as a speaker for The Middle East Forum, a
right-wing organization which had openly declared its support for an invasion.
In May 2004 the New York Times published an editorial which stated that
its journalism in the build-up to war had "sometimes been lax". In the many
situations in which Miller used Chalabi and other Iraqi exiles as her sources
for the stories about weapons of mass destruction, the New York Times was
more than lax, demonstrating a highly unprofessional approach to investigative journalism. One colleague referred to Miller's journalism as "wacky assed",
and Slate reporter Jack Shafer asked, after one of her "explosive" articles, "Is the
New York Times breaking the news- or flaking for the military?" Shafer wrote
in great detail about Miller's "record of error" in promoting Bush's war, and

said, "Miller, more than any other reporter, showcased the Weapons of Mass Destruction speculations and intelligence 'findings' by the Bush administration". **60.**

Following several articles by Miller's colleagues at the New York Times, David Lindorf wrote in Counterpunch.com; "Without outright calling their co-worker a liar and a shill for the Bush administration's war marketing campaign, they left no doubt in the reader's mind that this is what she was, and that the Times senior management and many of her colleagues at the paper thought exactly the same thing". **61.**

On May 27, 2003, a secret <u>Defense Intelligence Agency</u> fact-finding mission in Iraq reported unanimously to intelligence officials in Washington that two trailers captured in Iraq by Kurdish troops "had nothing to do with biological weapons." The trailers had been a key part of the argument for the 2003 invasion. Secretary of State Colin Powell had told the United Nations Security Council, "We have first-hand descriptions of biological weapons factories on wheels and on rails." The Pentagon team was sent to investigate the trailers after the invasion, and the team of experts unanimously found "no connection to anything biological". One of the experts told reporters that they privately called the trailers "the biggest sand toilets in the world." The White House continued to refer to the trailers as "mobile biological laboratories" throughout the year, despite knowing that they had not produced a single biological weapon. A <u>Washington Post</u> article on April 12, 2006 disclosed some of the details of the report. According to the Post:

"The survey group's final report in September 2004 – 15 months after the technical report was written – said the trailers were impractical for biological weapons production and were almost certainly intended for manufacturing hydrogen for weather balloons."

The information about mobile biological weapons labs emanated from an Iraqi in exile nicknamed Curveball who was living in Germany and peddling false information to German security people. He was an alcoholic, with serious psychological issues, and the German agents after passing on this information warned the CIA that none of his claims were verified by other sources and were not credible. The German agents were astounded when the information from

Curveball made it into George Bush's State of the Union Address to Congress and into Colin Powell's infamous address to the UN Security Council on February 5, 2003. It is a criminal offense to lie to Congress, but this detail rarely imposed limitations on the behavior of Bush and Cheney.

On July 2, 2004, an article published by The Associated Press and Fox News reported that sarin gas warheads were found in South Central Iraq by Polish allies. The Polish troops secured these munitions on June 23, 2004, but it turned out that the warheads did not in fact contain sarin gas but "were all empty and tested negative for any type of chemicals". They dated back to the first Gulf War. It eventually transpired that the Poles, ever-willing to earn the bribes thrown its way by the Bush government, had bought the shells from Iraqis for $5,000 each, and then had used these phony shells to create a fabricated 'weapons of mass destruction' story. This and other fictitious accounts of supposed weapons of mass destruction were the basis for the mendacious Bush claim that the weapons of mass destruction had been found.

On October 6, 2004, the head of the Iraq Survey Group (ISG), Charles Duelfer, announced to the US Senate Armed Service Commission that the group found no evidence that Iraq under Saddam Hussein had produced and stockpiled any weapons of mass destruction since 1991, when UN sanctions were imposed. In fact, the many documents recovered in Bagdad showed that Saddam did not consider Iraq to be an enemy of the USA and hoped at some point that Iraq could resume normal relations with the United States. All of his weapons acquisition programs going back to the 1980's were motivated by his enmity for Iran, and by his desire to counter-balance the ominous military threat posed by Israel. The United States abandoned its search for WMDs in Iraq on January 12, 2005. The U.S.-sponsored search for WMD had at that point used 1200 inspectors and cost taxpayers over $1 billion, an exorbitant sum considering that Bush and Cheney had absolutely no evidence that weapons of mass destruction had ever existed.

John Prados wrote:

"The (war) planners knew that Iraqi WMD programs were either nascent, moribund or non-existent, exactly the opposite of the President's repeated message to the American people. Actual intelligence was consistently distorted, manipulated and ignored in service of a particular enterprise under false pretenses. Americans have been shamed. Americans do not like to think of themselves as aggressors, but raw aggression is what took place in Iraq." **62.**

In an interview with BBC in June 2004, David Kay, former head of the Iraq Survey Group, made the following comment:

"Anyone out there holding – as I gather Prime Minister Blair has recently said – the prospect that, in fact, the Iraq Survey Group is going to unmask actual weapons of mass destruction, [is] really delusional."

Despite the best efforts of Cheney and Rumsfeld, who insisted that their torturers find evidence of collaboration between Saddam and al Qaeda, thus invoking the unproductive and highly illegal "enhanced interrogation techniques", none were found.

The 9/11 Commission Report stated:

"We have seen no evidence that any Iraq/al-Qaeda contacts ever developed into a collaborative operational relationship. Nor have we seen evidence indicating that Iraq cooperated with al-Qaeda in developing or carrying out any attacks on the United States."

This report directly contradicted what Bush said in a State of the Union address to Congress after the invasion of Iraq. Bush stated "We have removed an ally of al Qaeda and cut off a source of terrorist funding." Bush made this statement at a time when the White House had no evidence whatsoever that Saddam had any connection to Al Qaeda, and no evidence that Iraq was a state sponsor of terrorism. Richard Clarke in an interview on March 21, 2004, stated that "there's absolutely no evidence that Iraq was supporting al-Qaeda, ever". The Bush family friends in Saudi Arabia were far more active in the terrorist business than Saddam ever was.

According to terrorism specialist Peter Bergen, President Bush "is right that Iraq is a main front in the war on terrorism, but this is a front that we created." Bush turned Iraq from a nation that was no threat to the United States into a breeding ground for anti-American hatred. Terrorist attacks tripled in the time between the invasion, and 2004. When Donald Rumsfeld said he needed "metrics" on whether America was winning or losing the war on terror, Bergen suggested that "an exponentially rising number of terrorist attacks is one metric that seems relevant". Terrorist attacks recently in Paris, and in San Bernardino, California, gave proof to that response. **63.**

In casting about for excuses to launch their illegal invasion of Iraq, "regime change" became a term that was offered by Bush and Cheney repeatedly, hoping that if they said it often enough, the phrase would almost sound legal. Lord Goldsmith, Attorney General in England and legal advisor to Tony Blair, advised Blair that given "the patent criminality of regime change" as a motive for invasion, it would be necessary to create other conditions by which the USA and UK could legally support military action. **64.**

Former Secretary of State and national security advisor Henry Kissinger spoke out about regime change. He said:

"Regime change as a goal for military intervention challenges the international system established by the 1648 Treaty of Westphalia, which, after the carnage of the religious wars, established the principle of non-intervention in the domestic affairs of other states. And the notion of justified pre-emption runs counter to modern international law, which sanctions use of force in self-defence only against actual, not potential, threats." **65.**

Jim Webb, former Reagan secretary of the Navy and decorated Marine combat hero, said, "Unilateral wars designed to bring about regime change and a long-term occupation should be undertaken only when a nation's existence is clearly at stake." **66.**

UK Foreign Secretary Jack Straw sent a secret letter to Prime Minister Tony Blair in April 2002 warning Blair that the case for military action against Iraq was of "dubious legality." The letter goes on to state that "regime change per se is no justification for military action" and that "the weight of legal advice here is that a fresh [UN] mandate may well be required." **67.**

At the time that Bush started using "regime change" as a rationale to explain the invasion, there were many dictators around the world who were brutal, tyrannical and oppressive. That Saddam was these things was beyond dispute, but not remotely sufficient to justify starting a war. Saddam was in fact the American choice for leader of Iraq, and was supported by the White House through his worst atrocities.

Alan Cowell wrote in the New York Times:

"Washington and its allies held the strikingly unanimous view that whatever the sins of the Iraqi leader, he offered the West and the region a better hope for his country's stability than did those who have suffered his repression". **68.**

Reporter John King wrote that during the 1980's the United States sold Iraq chemicals and other goods for Iraq's chemical and biological weapons programs. The CIA and the Defense Intelligence Agency supplied Iraq with information to help its forces use chemical weapons against Iran's troops, causing the deaths of 50,000 Iranian soldiers. **69.** The United States then used its veto power to block UN Security Council resolutions condemning Iraq's use of illegal chemical weapons as a violation of the Geneva Convention (1925). Even when the United States knew that Saddam was using those weapons on his own people, the Kurds, the U.S. continued to send weapons-grade anthrax, cyanide and other chemical and biological weapons to Iraq. **70.** Donald Rumsfeld, while working for the Reagan administration, was a key figure in helping Iraq obtain and use those 'weapons of mass destruction'.

Bush used these chemical attacks as justification for war, even though these attacks had been sponsored by the US military. His penchant for prevarication surfaced once again when he stated that 20,000 Kurds were killed by chemical assaults in Halabja by Saddam's military. In fact there were fewer than 8000 Kurds killed in that attack, a far cry from the number of Iranians killed by American chemical weapons in the Iran-Iraq war. **71.** Bush constantly exaggerated certain statistics, while ignoring others that were less "appropriate", when trying to sell his war to the American public.

In looking around the world for more appropriate candidates for regime change, the most obvious choice would have been to send troops to Darfur, in southern Sudan, where the Arab-dominated government was killing hundreds of thousands of black Africans. **72.** A second excellent choice would have been the brutal government of Kim Jong-il in North Korea. He repeatedly imprisoned, tortured and killed all of his political rivals. Going to prison in North Korea for any reason was a precursor to torture and execution. North Korea has been constantly taunting the South with attacks across the border, and even shelled a South Korean patrol boat, killing a number of South Korean sailors. Despite his people living in near-starving conditions, despite the many outrageous brutalities committed by his family, despite North Korea being part of Bush's "axis of evil", despite Kim Jong-il's many threats to the USA and to South Korea, and despite the development of a nuclear weapons program in defiance of the UN, Kim Jong-il's North Korea was never considered for "regime change". Maybe it had something to do with North Korea, like the Sudan, not having vast quantities of oil, or not being in a geographic position of strategic importance in the Middle East. Or maybe it was because North Korea has a standing army of over 1,500,000 soldiers, one of the largest in the world. Bullies like the USA try to pick on smaller, more defenseless countries like Iraq, that can't fight back.

Zimbabwe with Robert Mugabe at the helm would be yet another example of a despotic government in need of regime change. He has been running phony elections, jailing and killing his political rivals, overseeing the brutal take-over of white-owned plantations and the vicious murders of the owners by gangs of marauders. Under Mugabe's rule, Zimbabwe went from being a relatively well-off country and a net exporter of food, to being a net importer of food, with insane levels of inflation, a stagnant economy, high unemployment and levels of graft and corruption that bordered on the absurd. Zimbabwe would have been an excellent choice for regime change, had that been the motive for military action. But Zimbabwe has no oil, and like North Korea and the Sudan is not located in a geographic position from which to militarily dominate the oil-rich Middle East.

Yet another excellent case for "regime change" right there in the Middle East would have been Saudi Arabia, like Iraq loaded with oil. This radical Islamic state with its missionary zeal is one of the most extreme fundamentalist nations in the world. It is spreading its style of radical Islam to Pakistan, and to other countries, and has consistently supported and funded terrorist activities around the world. An oppressive dictatorship since 1931, the House of Saud has brutalized its people for years. In one instance of extreme brutality in 1979, a group of 200 religious zealots took over the Great Mosque in Mecca, in an effort to move the government towards a more traditional interpretation of Islam. The government reacted by taking 60 of the religious protesters to their home towns. They forced their families, friends and neighbors out into the street, where they had to watch while each of these political protesters was publically beheaded. More recently, the Saudi kingdom beheaded 47 of its citizens, including several who did nothing more than advocate for human rights for the Shiite minority. With all of the publicity surrounding ISIS beheading its prisoners, America's client state and the Bush family's best friend Saudi Arabia leads the world in beheading its citizens.

"What happens in Crawford stays in Crawford."
—Jay Leno

Going beyond that violence and barbarism, 15 of the 19 hijackers who perpetrated the 9/11 attacks on the twin towers in New York were from Saudi Arabia, as was Osama bin Laden. When the 9/11 investigation commission tried to contact the families of these 15 hijackers and interview them, they were blocked by the Saudi government, which refused investigators access to any Saudi Arabian citizens. You would think that this alone would be more than enough rationale for regime change. But Osama bin Laden's family were closely involved as investors in The Carlyle Group, a multi-national corporation based in America with strong ties to the military-industrial complex. Coincidentally, George Bush Sr. was on the Board of Directors of The Carlyle Group. Bush Sr. has been feted in Saudi Arabia on several occasions by government leaders, and Saudi government representatives have been visitors at George Jr's ranch in Texas. Saudi Arabia owns over 7% of the American economy, with $860 billion in investments in American corporations and over $1trillion deposited in American banks. It would cause a serious financial convulsion if Saudi Arabia were offended in any way and decided to divest itself of its ownership in America's economy. Maybe that explains why, in the days immediately following 9/11, one of the first planes to fly out of the United States was the plane taking the Bin Laden family back to Saudi Arabia, without any of them being questioned in regard to the twin towers disaster.

"Regime change" was a criminal action, a violation of international law, and a hoax. It was a weak and flailing attempt by a team of compulsive liars in the White House to justify their cruel assault on the sovereign nation of Iraq. It was one in a series of mendacious fabrications that led to the final rationale, the mission to "bring democracy to the Middle East".

The United States has never encouraged or supported democracy worldwide, unless it fit a particular national objective. Support for such despotic dictators as Pinochet in Chile, Marcos in the Philippines, Duvalier in Haiti, the Shah in Iran, Ceausecu in Romania, Suharto in Indonesia and the brutal, racist apartheid regime in South Africa, is but a small sample of America's assault on democracy worldwide. More contemporarily, at the same time that Bush was proclaiming the vital need for democracy in Iraq, he was supporting brutal dictatorships in Kuwait, Egypt, Uzbekistan and Saudi Arabia. At the same time that Bush was preaching democracy promotion in the Middle East, he was also supporting a military coup in Venezuela to oust the democratically-elected government of Hugo Chavez.

That good friend of the Bush family, Saudi Arabia, is the antithesis of democracy, a brutal, totalitarian dictatorship that oppresses its female population, and leads the world in beheading its political activists. Yet America considers Saudi Arabia to be an important ally, and members of the House of Saud royal family are close personal friends with the Bush family, despite that country being an insult to democracy. Prince Bandar bin Sultan was so close to both George H. W. Bush and George Bush Jr. during his 23 years as Saudi ambassador to the United States that he was frequently referred to by members of the Bush family as "Bandar Bush". Few things can be more insulting to democratic values than watching George Bush walk hand-in-hand with members of the Saudi royal family, as they tour his ranch in Crawford, Texas.

In yet another American assault on democracy, when the USA went to Turkey and asked that country to help in the invasion of Iraq, a poll showed that 95% of the population of Turkey were opposed to any involvement in the invasion of Iraq. Because the government of Turkey supported the democratic wishes of a vast percentage of its people and declined involvement in Bush's illegal invasion, Turkey was insulted by the White House, who said Turkey's government was "lacking democratic credentials". Colin Powell called for sanctions against Turkey. Paul Wolfowitz, dedicated war hawk in Washington, berated the Turkish military for not intervening and coercing the government into compliance with U.S. demands. Wolfowitz "ordered" the government in Turkey to apologize.

Jose Maria Azner, Prime Minister of Spain, offered yet another example of America's approach to democracy. He went to a summit in the Azores with Bush and Blair and declared his support for the invasion. A poll in Spain at that time showed that 2% of his citizens agreed with his support for Bush's war. For this Azner was called the "hope for democracy".

This democracy deficit exists not only with America's approach to foreign countries but also at home in America today. After the invasion of Iraq a poll showed that a large majority of Americans wanted Iraq to be handed over to the U.N. The results of this poll were never published in any of the mainstream media, and this action was never considered by the Bush government. In yet another outrage against democratic values, in the election of 2000, Florida and its governor, George's brother Governor Jeb Bush, knocked 80,000 potential Democrat voters off the register. In one voters' poll 16,000 legitimate votes for Al Gore weren't counted while 4000 totally fictitious votes for George Bush were counted. This was a major story on BBC in England, and in other media outlets around the world, yet wasn't reported in the mainstream media in the USA until 7 months after the election. What could be more troubling to America than knowing that its democratic process had been abused?

Craig Unger in his book The Fall of the House of Bush discussed America's enigmatic relationship with democracy. He said:

"The world's greatest constitutional democracy had implemented unprecedented secrecy and spying on its own citizens. There had been a dramatic erosion of civil liberties. The creation of a Soviet-style gulag at Guantanamo made a mockery of America's Constitution by suspending habeas corpus and embracing the detention of prisoners- allowing them no rights whatsoever. The presidency itself has become an "imperial presidency", consolidating enormous powers far beyond those intended by the founding fathers, effectively gutting the concepts of checks and balances." 73.

Bush never wanted democracy in Iraq. What he and Cheney and the rest of his regime wanted was the installation of a government under U.S. control with a democratic facade and nothing more. That was the <u>Project for Iraq in the 21st Century</u>. Noam Chomsky in his book "Perilous Power" wrote, "They support democracy if and only if it conforms to U.S. economic and strategic objectives". 74.

Hypocrisy was but one of the many descriptors that would identify the war hawks in the Bush regime who continually emphasized their narrow-minded objective to invade Iraq, overthrow Saddam, and make that country a client state of America. Paul Wolfowitz was one of the most aggressive hawks in the Bush government and also one of the leading hypocrites. Wolfowitz stated after the invasion, "I think all foreigners should stop interfering in the internal affairs of Iraq." Wolfowitz clearly did not see the bitter irony in his ultimate hypocrisy. Wolfowitz was not the only one guilty of hypocrisy, in the lead-up to the invasion of Iraq.

George Bush is a born-again Christian. A few years ago, born-again Christians were displaying bracelets and other advertisements with the acronym "WWJD". The idea was that in times of moral crisis, they were to ask themselves, "What Would Jesus Do?" Did George Bush look into his soul, when he was preparing to invade Iraq, and ask himself that question? Why was it that media pundits never asked him that question? Why was it that Bush was never asked about the glaring contradiction between his "born-again" Christianity and his immoral, unethical and blood-thirsty war in Iraq, the war that killed 210,000 innocent civilians? The president met with conservative, pro-war Christians (now there is an oxymoron) about the pre-emptive strike on Iraq on several occasions leading up to his invasion, but he refused to meet with bishops of the Methodist church or with the National Council of Churches, and he refused the advice of the Pope, because they were all opposed to his war. A coalition of over 60 religious groups from the United States and Great Britain issued a declaration condemning the idea of pre-emptive war because of religious, moral and practical grounds. Bush ignored their declaration.

Coming to NBC this fall:

The White House: Criminal Intent

PunditKitchen.com

Jesus Christ did not stand as a symbol for any kind of war, and it would be unimaginable that He would support an aggressive, predatory and bloodthirsty war that killed over 1,200,000 people and destroyed a country's entire infrastructure. Imagine Jesus of the Christian Bible overseeing the torture protocols at Guantanamo, or supervising the disgusting behavior of American troops at Abu Ghraib, or ordering the mass slaughter of women and children in Fallujah. Rather than listening to the words of Jesus Christ from the Bible, Bush must have been listening instead to Voltaire, a French writer and philosopher, who once said: "It is forbidden to kill: therefore all murderers are punished...unless they kill in large numbers and to the sound of trumpets."

George Bush is a pretentious Christian and a situational Christian, a mass murderer and a war criminal, and his values coincided with the Christian Bible only when it was convenient for him. When he was on the warpath, hell-bent on wholesale slaughter, with plunder as his primary goal, then his Christianity was conveniently set aside. In response to Bush's twisted version of Christian values, Glenn Greenwald said:

"The same president who has insisted that core moralism drives him has brought America to its lowest moral standing in history." 75.

Larry Johnson, deputy director of the State Department's Office of Counter Terrorism, was a registered Republican in 2000. He voted for George Bush and donated to his election campaign. In February 2004 he said:

"By April of last year I was beginning to pick up grumblings from friends inside the intelligence community that there had been pressure applied to analysts to come up with certain conclusions. In an email exchange with another friend I raised the possibility that the Bush administration had bought into a lie. My friend, who works within the intelligence community, challenged me on the use of the word 'bought', and suggested instead that the Bush administration had created the lie. We know now that most of the reasons we were given for going to war were wrong." **76.**

Zbigniew Brzezinski worked as U.S. National Security Advisor for the Carter administration, and worked also for Presidents Lyndon Johnson, Ronald Reagan and George H. W. Bush. He is a recipient of the Presidential Medal of Freedom. After the invasion of Iraq he said, "The evocative symbol of America in the eyes of much of the world ceases to be the Statue of Liberty and instead has become the prison camp at Guantanamo." **77.**

Many observers from around the world were amazed that Bush and his regime could sell such an obviously phoney rationale for war to the American people, given the highly-respected investigative powers of the mainstream media in the USA. But critics saw the majority of the newspapers and major TV networks become feverishly patriotic after 9/11, causing an alarming lack of critical scrutiny in regard to the proposed war. Many media representatives actually boasted of the prejudice in their reporting, taking pride in their total disdain for investigative journalism. One reporter stated on television, "You're damn right I'm biased" and another said "When my country is at war, I want my country to win", thus justifying his prejudicial reporting. At the expense of investigative journalism, reporters were instead lobbing softball questions at Bush and his regime members, and rarely followed up when Bush's devious answers were either evasive or off-topic. The behavior of the media provided the perfect setting for Bush to perpetrate his deceptions and prevarications, and push his nation into a totally unnecessary war.

Jimmy Breslin, author and media pundit, said of the lead-up to the invasion of Iraq:

"America witnessed the worst failure to inform the public that we have seen; the Pekingese of the press run clip-clop along the hall to the next press conference." **78.**

Respected war correspondent Christiane Amanpour in an interview with Tina Brown of CNBC said:

"My station was intimidated by the Administration and its foot-soldiers at Fox News. It put a climate of fear and self-censorship in terms of the kind of broadcast work we did." **79.**

George Will was among the many media sycophants who shilled for the Bush administration, stating, "Hussein has vowed revenge. He has anthrax, he loves biological weapons, he has terrorist training camps, including 747's to practice on." Everything he said in that statement was a lie. **80.**

Laurie Mylroie wrote a guest editorial published on April 2, 2004 in the Wall Street Journal titled <u>Very Awkward Facts</u> that blamed Saddam Hussein and Iraq as the state sponsor for the 9/11 attacks on the Twin Towers and the Pentagon. Despite the fact that all credible intelligence analysts had dismissed any connection between al Qaeda and Saddam Hussein, her specious theory was cited and given credence by The Washington Post, CBS News, ABC, Fox News, U.S. News and World Report, CNN, The Times (London) and the Dallas Morning News, among more than 100 news outlets that repeatedly referred to her fallacious article. **81.**

At the same time, Bob Simon of CBS News lamented, "We are no longer a news-gathering organization." **82.** Many of the highest-profile journalists relied almost entirely on press releases handed to them by the White House, or press releases from defense contractors. Dana Millbank, the Washington Post's White House correspondent, said about his reporter's job covering the Bush Administration: "It's become more of a stenographic kind of job." **83.**

One major defense contractor, General Electric, made billions from the war in Iraq. GE owns MSNBC and in the lead-up to the invasion of Iraq GE arbitrarily cancelled popular TV host Phil Donahue's show because he had featured "too many" anti-war guests. While GE was censoring Phil Donahue, a veritable parade of retired military generals was employed by Fox, CNN and NBC to parrot Pentagon talking points given to them by their military handlers. Each of these ex-generals was employed by a defense contractor who subsequently earned obscene profits from the war in Iraq. Despite their obvious bias, they were actually believed by the American public, supposedly verifying, through their lies the many untruthful statements that Bush and his regime members perpetrated to justify this fiasco of a war.

The Washington Post after Powell's mendacious address at the U.N. said his evidence was "irrefutable" in making the case for war. In fact, virtually everything he said was refuted and proven not to be true. In the months leading up to the invasion of Iraq, the Washington Post wrote 140 front page articles making the Bush case for war, and its editors wrote 27 editorials supporting war with Iraq. Meanwhile, when British intelligence officer Katherine Gunn exposed the Bush government for spying on U.N. delegates and pressuring then to support the war, the Washington Post ignored that story, as did the rest of the mainstream media.

The Denver Post after Powell's address to the U.N. called him "Marshal Dillon facing down a gunslinger in Dodge City". and said he had shown the world "not just one smoking gun but a battery of them." What Powell had actually shown the world was how easily a country could be duped into supporting an illegal and totally unnecessary war.

Craig Unger in his book <u>The Fall of the House of Bush</u> describes Walter Isaacson, chairman and C.E.O. of CNN, telling <u>Bill Moyer's Journal</u>; "There was a real sense that you don't get that critical of a government that's leading us in wartime. Big people in corporations were calling up and saying, 'you're being anti-American here....'"

Said one astute observer:

"In the process of making the mainstream media acquiescent and subservient to the White House, Bush and his neocons have attacked the integrity and demeaned the sincerity of the media in America, and have made the news inconsequential for generations of young Americans."

Glenn Greenwald, in his book "No Place to Hide", said of the mainstream media:

"Especially since 9/11 the U.S. media has been jingoistic and intensely loyal to the government, and thus hostile, sometimes viciously so, to anyone who exposed its secrets." **84.**

The culpability of the mainstream media in promoting and encouraging this despicable war was no more in evidence than in its reaction to presentations at the United Nations by Hans Blix and Mohammed ElBaradei. Blix, the chief U.N. weapons inspector, gave a presentation in which he contradicted key aspects of the Bush case for war. He had scoured Iraq since the fall of 2002 and had found no evidence of chemical or biological weapons. ElBaradei testified that he had found no evidence of a nuclear weapons program. Together with the many doubts expressed by America's intelligence agencies, the reports by Blix and ElBaradei seemingly would give pause to the Bush regime's rush to war. When Bush and his neocon war hawks refused to back down, over 10 million people marched in protest around the world, including over 500,000 in New York City. **85.**

The mainstream media virtually ignored these virulent protests, and continued to cheer on Bush and Cheney in their march to disaster. Rather than actually investigating the many lies and deceits of Bush and Cheney in their promotion of a war agenda, the media in America became obsessed instead with labeling war critics as unpatriotic. When Congressman Jim McDermott returned from Iraq and stated that Bush was misleading the American people, he was labeled a "traitor" in the mainstream media. Scott Ritter went to Iraq and spoke at the Iraqi National Assembly and the media responded by stating that "aiding and abetting the enemy is treason". Phil Donahue was labeled a traitor and "The Prince of Darkness", Richard Perle, called The New Yorker's esteemed writer Seymour Hersh "the closest thing American journalism has to a terrorist" for speaking out against the war. Ted Kennedy was identified as part of the "treason lobby" and Senator Max Cleland, who lost 3 limbs in the Vietnam War, was called "traitorous" for suggesting a more cautious approach to war. Few people realized that the views expressed by these "traitorous liberals who aided and abetted the enemy" were strikingly similar to the views of George H. W. Bush and General Brent Scowcroft. **86.**

The mainstream media in the United States paved the way into Iraq for George W. Bush, justifying his outlaw behavior at every turn while selling out the whole concept of investigative journalism. Even less impressive was the Democrat opposition in Congress, who sold out to a perverted version of patriotism and acted as cheerleaders to the Republican mercenaries.

The invasion of Iraq was planned and prepared far outside the parameters of any consideration for weapons of mass destruction, regime change, Saddam's connections to al Qaeda or to the 9/11 attacks, Iraq being a state sponsor of terrorism, or America bringing democracy to the Middle East. Once all of these lies have been discounted, it is necessary to find the truth behind this awful invasion. Oil is an easy answer but that is only one of several factors that led to this war. The actual truth lies in the pervasive influence of cowboy culture in America and extends well beyond the oil fields. The bloodied gun culture still prevalent on U.S. streets today is but one of several characteristics that tie cowboy values to the invasion of Iraq. Just as in the cowboy movies of old, Bush divided his world into "good guys" and "bad guys", thus justifying the carnage that took place. He abused the law of the U.N. and of the World Court in La Hague, just as cowboys abused the law in the Old West. Bush used revenge as one of his primary motives, both on a personal level because of Saddam's attempt on his father's life and on a national level as "payback" for 9/11. Ultimately his final goal was money, one of the primary motivations that we see consistently in cowboy movies, and an overwhelming motivation in Iraq.

In the following chapter I will establish just how prevalent and how popular cowboy culture is in America today. Although the 'cowboy period' in American history was very short, encompassing no more than 35 years (1860-1895), it has had a profound and enduring effect on American culture. Many Americans see the iconic cowboy as a positive symbol of what it means to be American. But many around the world see him as a mercenary, arrogant bully, in particular after the Bush invasion of Iraq. It is this 2nd characterization that most quickly comes to mind when identifying with the 'war president' George W. Bush.

CHAPTER 3

....

THE INFLUENCE OF COWBOY
CULTURE IN AMERICA TODAY

....

"Europeans think, 'This guy doesn't sound smart. He sounds like the worst Hollywood cliché of the gun-slinging cowboy.' We find it hard to respect that."

— JONATHON FREEDLAND THE GUARDIAN (2002)

The history of the cowboy has its roots in the conquests of the Spanish conquistadores, who brought a tradition of open-range herding by horse-mounted drovers to the New World. By the year 1500 Spanish cowboys called vaqueros were raising cattle commercially in the Caribbean, and the first Spanish stock crossed to the North American mainland with Cortes and his conquistadors. Juan de Onate's men trailed more than 1000 head of cattle into the Rio Grande valley in 1598. 1. Later, mission friars built up large cattle herds in California and Texas. Much of the terminology and many of the skills used in cowboy culture came from the Spanish. Ranch came from the Spanish word "rancho", meaning farm. Terms like lariat, lasso, dogie and rodeo came from the Spanish language, and many of the cowboys in America in the early years of the 19th century were Mexican. The development of the western saddle and the saddle horn began with the Spanish ranchers as well, as did the "round-up", the practice of branding cows, and the traditional cattle drive. The Spanish influence on cowboy culture had its effect not only on the procedures involved in herding cattle, but also on the apparel. Cowboy hats, the chaps and spurs that they wore, and their other clothing had their beginnings in Spanish culture.

It was not until the end of the Civil War that the number of truly American cowboys began to rise and dominate the number of Mexicans working in the cattle business in the American west, and this time period became known as the "golden age" of the cowboy in America. It reached its apex in 1883, when cowboy and writer Teddy Blue Abbott, while trailing a herd from Texas to Montana, could survey the land on both sides of the Platte River and see 28 different herds of cattle on the trail. 2. With the new western railroads providing access to eastern markets, the cattle industry stretched from Texas to the Canadian prairies.

The Hispanic influence on cowboy culture was acknowledged in one of the greatest cowboy novels ever written, Lonesome Dove, by Larry McMurtry. In this story, based on the real-life exploits of Charles Goodnight and Oliver Loving, the protagonists, Augustus McRae and Captain Call, take a ragtag band of cowboys across the border on a regular basis to steal cattle and horses from the large Mexican ranches. Not to be outdone, the Mexican vaqueros rustle the cattle and horses from ranches in Texas and drive them south across the border to Mexico. In one rather comical scene from the movie, the Lonesome Dove cowboys drive a herd of stolen cattle and horses north, in the middle of the night, straight through a stolen herd that is being brought south by the Mexican vaqueros, thus framing the relationship between the American cowboy and the vaquero.

The fame of both the book Lonesome Dove and the TV movie Lonesome Dove speak volumes about the influence of cowboy culture in America. The Lonesome Dove novel won the Pulitzer Prize for fiction in 1986, and the movie was nominated for eighteen Emmy awards, winning seven. It also won two Golden Globe awards, and drew a huge viewing audience, having been seen in over 21 million households. In J. Marvin Hunter's The Trail Drivers of Texas Charles Goodnight wrote about his friend, Oliver Loving, and about the early years of driving cattle in the American West.

"Oliver Loving is undoubtedly the first man who ever trailed cattle from Texas. His earliest effort was in 1858 when he took a herd across the frontier of the Indian Nation through eastern Kansas and northwestern Missouri into Illinois. His second attempt was in 1859. He left the frontier on the upper Brazos and took a northwest course until he struck the Arkansas River, somewhere about the mouth of the Walnut, and followed it to just above Pueblo where he wintered. In 1867 we started another herd west over the same trail and struck the Pecos the latter part of June. After we had gone up this river about one hundred miles it was decided that Mr. Loving should go ahead on horseback in order to reach New Mexico and Colorado in time to bid on the contracts which were to be let in July, to use the cattle we then had on trail, for we knew that there were no other cattle in the West to take their place." **3.**

At a time when the western movie seemed to have lost its panache, Lonesome Dove revived the genre, paving the way for Best Picture academy awards for two other westerns in the next seven years, and a Best Picture nomination in 2012.

With the cattle drive boom during the latter half of the 19th century, the culture of the frontiersman became woven into the very fabric of American culture. Buffalo Bill Cody's Wild West Exhibition in 1883 marked the beginning of a new image of the cowboy as "young, white, and virile." Prentis Ingraham's novel, Buck Taylor, King of the Cowboys, Charlie Russell's paintings of cowboys, and Owen Wister's novel The Virginian also transformed the image of the cowboy from an illiterate, overworked cowhand to an idealized, romantic hero. **4.**

Legendary tales of the great cowboys of that time and their exploits were captured and authenticated in the many popular western novels that followed The Virginian. Written by such famous authors as Max Brand, Zane Grey and Louis L'Amour, these novels helped shape the heroic image of the American cowboy. Louis L'Amour sold over 300 million cowboy novels, a true testament to the influence of cowboy culture in American society. Kevin Costner grew up reading the western romance novels of Lauran Paine, and the classic western movie Open Range, which he produced, directed and starred in, was based on Paine's famous novel The Open Range Men.

Music was an integral part of cowboy culture, and the Grand Ol' Oprey in Nashville was at the core of this expanding influence. Country and western music quickly became main-stream, and its impact on American culture was undeniable. Many of the best-known and best-loved musicians, including Hank Snow, Hank Williams, Patsy Cline, Waylon Jennings, Loretta Lynn, Merle Haggard, Willie Nelson and Johnny Cash owe their fame and fortune to country and western music, one of the top-selling categories in the music industry today. In the process of establishing itself as an extremely popular genre in the music industry, country and western music reinforced the popularity of cowboy culture. The preferred style of dress for musicians while performing country and western music imitates the clothing worn by cowboys, with most wearing cowboy boots and cowboy hats. Many of the traditional themes of the heroic cowboy lifestyle were addressed in the music of the country and western stars. As Waylon Jennings so aptly put it, in his classic song <u>My Heroes Have Always Been Cowboys</u>:

"I grew up a-dreamin' of being a cowboy,

and lovin' the cowboy way.

Pursuin' the life of my high-riding heroes,

I burned up my childhood days.

I learned all the rules of the modern-day drifter.

Don't you hold onto nothin' too long.

Just take what you need from the ladies and leave them

With the words of a sad country song.

My heroes have always been cowboys

And they still are it seems.

Sadly in search of and one step in back of

Themselves and their slow-moving dreams"

Waylon Jennings was one of a score of popular country and western recording artists who found fame and fortune in the 1960's and 1970's. Jennings captured the loneliness of the cowboy lifestyle, the isolation, the individualism and the heroic nature of the cowboy. When Tim McGraw sang, "I guess that's just the cowboy in me," he was singing of the American heroic prototype - strong, brave, trustworthy, loyal and self-reliant. Groups like The Nitty Gritty Dirt Band and The Flying Burrito Brothers crossed the divide between country and rock, drawing country and western music more and more into the mainstream as they re-enforced that myth of the iconic American cowboy. No group achieved this cross-over effect more successfully than The Eagles, with their classic hit song <u>Desperado</u>. Don Henley sang, "Your pain and your hunger are driving you home. And freedom, oh freedom, that's just some people talkin'.

Your prison is walking through this world all alone" and in those lines he captured the loneliness and the isolation of the western cowboy.

Testifying to the popularity and power of the country and western genre, Garth Brooks has become one of the most successful recording artists of all time, giving proof to the assertion that this style of music is embedded in American culture. Such current country and western stars as Taylor Swift and Brad Paisley play to sold-out audiences all over North America, and country music festivals in the summer months draw huge crowds of supporters. Many large cities in North America have a country and western bar where people of all ages dress up as cowboys, listen to country and western music and dance the two-step or take part in line dancing.

Although the rodeo cowboy, the urban cowboy, and the cowboy depicted in country and western music have all expanded the cowboy myth by combining aspects of historical and fictional cowboys, the most significant impact on the strength and resilience of cowboy culture has come through the movie industry. Hollywood has been obsessed with cowboy movies since the days of silent films, and still today, so many years later, cowboy movies draw millions into theaters all over the world. The aforementioned <u>Open Range</u> was released in 2003 and earned over $70 million in box office receipts worldwide, including over $14 million the first week it opened. Most recently, Quentin Tarantino's unorthodox cowboy movie <u>Django Unchained</u> was nominated for best picture and four other academy awards in 2012. One of the stars of 'Django', Christoph Waltz, won an Academy Award for Best Supporting Actor, and this cowboy movie grossed over $425 million world-wide.

Beginning in its earliest years with the first Western megastar, Tom Mix, who began appearing in silent cowboy films in 1909, so many great Western actors and great Western movies appeared that it became a dominant genre in Hollywood. Cowboys portrayed in movie and television productions have expanded the cowboy myth through characters such as Wyatt Earp, Wild Bill Hickok and Billy the Kid, and through actors such as John Wayne, Gary Cooper, Randolph Scott, Joel McCrae, Roy Rogers, Gene Autry and Clint Eastwood. Roy Rogers made over one hundred cowboy movies, and Gene Autry made ninety. Most of the top male actors in Hollywood in the 1950s and 1960's played leading roles in cowboy movies, including Gregory Peck (<u>The Big Country</u>-1958), Spencer Tracy (<u>Broken Lance</u>-1954), Marlon

Brando (Viva Zapata-1952), Burt Lancaster (Gunfight at the OK Corral-1957), Rock Hudson and Kirk Douglas (The Last Sunset-1961), Yul Brynner, Steve McQueen and Charles Bronson (The Magnificent Seven-1960), William Holden, Ernest Borgnine and Robert Ryan (The Wild Bunch-1969) and Robert Redford and Paul Newman (Butch Cassidy and the Sundance Kid-1969). There were very few significant male actors in Hollywood in the 50's and 60's who didn't appear in at least one cowboy movie. Famous character actors like Slim Pickens, Strother Martin, Bruce Dern, Walter Brennan and Warren Oates made a career out of playing supporting actor roles in cowboy movies.

Eleven times cowboy movies have been nominated for the Best Picture Academy Award and three cowboy movies took home that award, Unforgiven (1992), Dances with Wolves (1990) and Cimarron (1930). Stagecoach (1939), The Alamo (1960) and Butch Cassidy and the Sundance Kid (1969) were all nominated for seven academy awards, and Butch Cassidy and the Sundance Kid won four. It is now preserved in the U.S. National Film Registry by the Library of Congress as "culturally, historically or aesthetically significant", as are eighteen other cowboy movies. Modern counter-culture movies that allude to cowboy culture, but are not traditional cowboy movies, have also had great critical and financial success, including Midnight Cowboy, Best Picture Academy Award winner in 1969, Brokeback Mountain, a film about two modern-day gay cowboys that was nominated in 2005 for 8 Academy Awards, and the animated cowboy film Rango, which won the Academy Award for Best Animated Feature in 2011.

The incredible amount of resilience shown by cowboy culture in America was demonstrated in the Washington Post in September of 2015 when Michael Miller wrote a two-page article titled, The Quest to Bury the Old West. The article is about a two-bit outlaw nicknamed "Billy the Kid", who died shortly after his 21st birthday. The sub-title for the article is "Billy the Kid's life and death hotly debated, more than 130 years later", and the following list of stories about his life is remarkable. Bill O'Reilly, the notorious war hawk from Fox News, devoted one episode of his TV series "Legends and Lies: The Real West" to Billy the Kid. Historian Robert Stahl recently said he was filing a lawsuit with the New Mexico Supreme Court to force the government to issue an official death certificate for Billy the Kid. Many movies have been made about his short life, including the most famous "Pat Garrett and Billy the Kid'. It was based in part on a book by Pat Garrett, about the life and death of Billy the Kid, written in 1882. Garret was a famous lawman at that time and claimed in his book that he killed Billy. An article in the Arizona Republic in 2006 discounted Garrett's version and said Billy the Kid lived out his years peacefully, using the alias John Miller. Award-winning author Larry McMurtry wrote <u>Anything for Billy</u> in 1989, over 100 years after Garrett's book, and many books, movies and stories about Billy the Kid were available to the public in the intervening years. There has been much public clamor about New Mexico issuing a formal pardon to Billy for the crimes that he supposedly committed, a promise that was reportedly made to him before his death in 1881. Governor Bill Richardson, after a lengthy investigation in 2010, decided not to issue an official death certificate or a pardon. Professor Stahl, meanwhile, wrote a detailed 28-page legal brief that he intends to introduce to the Supreme Court. The professor is a member of a group called "The Billy the Kid Outlaw Gang", organized to try and dispel false rumors about Billy the Kid's death.

Only a cursory glance at all of this amazing obsession with a two-bit outlaw killed 130 years ago, at the tender age of 21, gives us proof that cowboy culture is an intrinsic part of American culture today. The cowboy paradigm extends to the naming of many sports teams in America, the most famous being the Dallas Cowboys football team, and all of the University of Wyoming men's sports teams. The University of Wyoming women's teams are called Cowgirls. The cowboy image is a regular feature in the world of advertising, and was used for years to sell Marlboro cigarettes. George W. Bush was not the first president to take on the cowboy persona, and use it to sell his presidential aspirations, for Ronald Reagan (coincidentally also a draft dodger, during World War 2) established his image as a cowboy president also in his sales pitch to the nation. The cowboy period in American history lasted barely 35 years, and ended well over 100 years ago, yet the cowboy continues to be a significant symbol in American culture today. **5.**

Cowboy movies have had an overwhelming influence on American culture over the past 100 years, both in terms of the incredible amount of money involved in the making and selling of these movies, and in the value system that has become an integral part of American culture. Americans have been inculcated with the belief system inherent in traditional cowboy culture, and this influence has had a significant effect on American behavior, in particular when identified with George Bush and his invasion of Iraq.

George Bush became president of the United States in 2001, and he brought to the White House a character and a wardrobe that were saturated with cowboy values. He had his $300 designer cowboy boots, his Levis, his $1,000 cowboy hat, his carefully-cultivated "aw shucks" Texas drawl, his cowboy "swagger" and he rode around his 1,600 acre Prairie Chapel Ranch in Texas assuming the nostalgic role of the western cowboy. More than that, he had the cowboy values that permeated his childhood. He grew up watching Gunsmoke, Bonanza, The Lone Ranger, The Roy Rogers Show and Gene Autry, shows that were on television every night. Cowboy films released by Hollywood were a regular feature of Saturday afternoon at the movies. There were so many cowboy movies released by Hollywood in the 1950's that the cowboy movie became a dominant genre, and these movies became a reflection of the values inherent in American culture. The cowboy that was George W. Bush's vicarious paradigm had a unique set of frontier values that included self-reliance, individualism, hard work, heroism and the overwhelming passion to "do what needs to be done".

In the months leading up to the war with Iraq, commentators began to portray Bush as a sheriff in the Old West who would go after the "evil-doers" alone, without a posse if need be, in order to defeat what he saw as lawlessness. In an address to the nation on March 17, 2003, George W. Bush declared, "Saddam Hussein and his sons must leave Iraq within 48 hours. Their refusal to do so will result in military conflict, commenced at a time of our choosing." The ultimatum aroused an immediate reaction in editorials and news articles that depicted George W. Bush as a cowboy sheriff who told the outlaws to get out of town or face a "showdown".

On March 19 Reuters ran a story titled "High Noon for Cowboy Era", in which the lead sentence declared that Bush's ultimatum was a throwback to the Wild West. Many times the cowboy metaphor was used when news pundits discussed Bush, and his obsession with invading Iraq and deposing Saddam Hussein. Bush himself encouraged such analogies, spraying his hackneyed cowboy clichés across Washington's landscape. His rhetoric in the lead-up to the Iraqi war was laden with frontier idiom, including when he said he would "ride herd" over objectionable Middle Eastern governments and "smoke out" America's enemies. He branded Saddam Hussein's government "an outlaw regime" and in referring to Osama Bin Laden, Bush declared "I want justice. And there's an old poster out West, I recall, that says, 'Wanted: Dead or Alive; it doesn't matter to me." He was framing his rhetoric in the language of outlaw wanted posters from old cowboy movies. When talking about the growing number of terrorists lining up against the United States, Bush said, "Bring 'em on!" One observer stated, "The incessant use of such language drew some smirks, mocked as the simplistic moral code of a cowboy."

Britain's newspaper The Guardian said on its editorial page "such language feeds the image overseas of Mr. Bush as a hopelessly inarticulate, trigger-happy cowboy." Piers Morgan, editor of London's Daily Mirror said "I think people look at him [Bush] and think John Wayne. We in Europe like John Wayne, we liked him in cowboy films. We don't like him running the world." Les Payne, writing for Newsday.com, extended the image of the cowboy riding into town with big guns in his critique of President Bush, who "acted like one of the cold-blooded, bloodthirsty Texas lawmen" who are eager to dispense justice. Payne called attention to Bush's tendency towards beaded eyes and finger pointing, which Payne claimed impeded U.S. diplomacy. Bush would attack Iraq, Payne asserted, in order to show that he was not "all hat and no cattle." Bush was portrayed as a crazed, egotistic Texas Ranger, eager to shoot with reckless abandon in the name of justice. Time magazine at one point called his foreign policy "cowboy diplomacy".

"THINGS DIDN'T GO ACCORDING TO PLAN." ~ GEORGE W. BUSH

In the case of the lead up to the war with Iraq, several political pundits made the point that comparisons of Bush to a heroic cowboy may have propelled the U.S. into the war in a faster and more determined way than might otherwise have been the case. The late Christopher Hitchens, a Vanity Fair writer and frequent analyst on televised news editorial programs, provided perhaps the most thorough analysis of the use of the cowboy myth, with a provocative examination of the contrast between U.S. and European attitudes towards that myth. Europeans, who would not join the posse to defeat the outlaw, were compared to timid saloonkeepers and shopkeepers, afraid to confront evil and afraid of the sheriff, who might shoot up the town while getting his man. Those fussy Europeans were caught up in such antiquated values as the Magna Carta, the protocols established at Nuremburg, the Geneva conventions and the UN charter. **6.** Eventually, the sheriff realized he had to ride out without a big posse, and outside the boundaries of international law, in order to "do what needs to be done".

The cowboy myth was widely used in the U.S. press in referring to Bush and his attitude, more often than not with positive connotations. But former Vice

President Al Gore used it to condemn Bush's policies on Iraq. Speaking in California, Gore argued that Bush should be focusing on the war on terror first before engaging with Iraq. After the speech, Gore told reporters that the Bush Administration had adopted a "do-it-alone, cowboy-type reaction to foreign affairs," and said "before you ride out after Jesse James, you ought to put the posse together." 7. Bush acknowledged and repeatedly fed into this cowboy image, including at a NATO conference in 2002 when in response to the posse allusions he said: "Contrary to my image as a Texan with two guns at my side, I'm more comfortable with a posse." 8.

After September 11, 2001, as editorial writers and public figures discussed terrorism more vigorously, they frequently described Bush using cowboy rhetoric and cowboy values. When Bush said things like "my preference is 'home on the range' rather than Commander-in-Chief" or "Some folks look at me and see a certain swagger, which in Texas is called walking", he merely reinforced all of the clichés about his cowboy identity and cowboy values. By examining these values in detail, we can see a direct connection between what cowboy movies teach us, and why George Bush chose to invade Iraq.

There are five predominant values that run through virtually all cowboy movies, and each of these values has its parallel in American culture. Because these five values are an inherent part of American culture, and an essential part of the Bush character, they also help to explain the decision-making process that resulted in the invasion of Iraq.

The first and most obvious value prevalent in all cowboy movies is that gun violence is an appropriate and viable resolution to conflict. Just as in American society today, cowboy culture encouraged the use of gun violence to resolve disputes. Cowboy movies have given us the distinct impression that most conflicts were resolved with guns in the Old West, just as guns are used routinely in America today to resolve differences.

The second value in every cowboy movie is that the world is made up of good guys and bad guys. Categorizing your enemy as bad guys, or evildoers, rationalizes and justifies the violence that takes place. Killing becomes accepted practice when good guys/bad guys is the black-and-white framework, and this cowboy rhetoric rolled with ease off the tongue of George Bush while he was promoting his mercenary war.

A third value prevalent in most cowboy movies involves a certain attitude bordering on contempt towards the law. In cowboy movies the law is a nebulous entity and can be used or abused to suit one's purposes. In the same way that Wyatt Earp manipulated and abused the law in Tombstone, George Bush manipulated and abused international law, the law of the United Nations and his own Constitution, when he invaded Iraq.

A fourth value that is seen in most cowboy movies, and in many aspects of American life, is revenge. After the hijacked airliners slammed into the twin towers, attacks of vandalism and personal assaults on American citizens who looked even remotely like they were from the Middle East became rampant. This was revenge. For many Americans, simply killing Muslims, whether at home or in Iraq, was revenge, despite no connection between 9/11 and Saddam Hussein. George Bush wanted personal revenge for Saddam trying to kill his father, and stated this publicly on several occasions, saying "he tried to kill my Dad". Revenge is a common theme in America for murders in the workplace, in the family and at school. Revenge acts as a viable and consistent rationale for violence in cowboy movies, it promotes violence in American culture, and it was a prime motivation for impelling Bush to order an attack on Iraq.

The fifth value that runs through most cowboy movies, and through much of American culture, is that money is the single most important goal in life. Acquisition of wealth is usually behind most of the killing in cowboy movies. Cascading piles of cold, hard cash symbolize what Iraq meant to America. Iraq has the second largest oil reserves in the world after Saudi Arabia, and America wanted that oil to keep its industrial empire operational. More than that, war with Iraq kept the trillion dollar military-industrial complex well-greased and ready to deal enormous profits to George Bush and his friends, the rich and powerful in America.

More than any other rationale, it is these five values as they are replicated in Hollywood's cowboy movies that underscore why America's cowboy president chose to invade the sovereign nation of Iraq. Each of these values explains this invasion, for without any of them the invasion of Iraq would never have happened. If violence wasn't such an immediate and acceptable recourse in America, there would have been no war. If Bush didn't rally public support with his many "evil-doer" and "good vs evil" speeches, there would have been no war. If Bush and his administration had respected the law of the U.N., the Nuremburg protocols, the Geneva conventions or even his own constitution, there would have been no war. If the American people and George Bush himself had not been obsessed with revenge, there would have been no war. Finally, if there hadn't been an obscene, trillion profit to be made from this war, it would never have happened. Any one of these factors, had it not been present, would have negated the momentum needed to sell this illegal and mercenary war to the American people. Each of these factors is predominant in cowboy movies, and in contemporary American culture, and it is these five values that led George Bush into his disastrous war in Iraq.

These values can be seen clearly in the five most famous Hollywood movies produced in the last 50 years, and these movies will be used to develop the parallel between the values inherent in cowboy movies and the rationale for invading Iraq. The five movies include <u>Open Range</u>, with Kevin Costner and Robert Duvall, <u>Unforgiven</u>, with Clint Eastwood, Gene Hackman and Morgan Freeman, <u>Tombstone</u> with Kurt Russell and Val Kilmer, <u>Butch Cassidy and the Sundance Kid</u>, with Robert Redford and Paul Newman, and <u>Django Unchained</u>, starring Jamie Foxx, Leonardo DiCaprio and Christoph Waltz.

Each of these movies featured Hollywood's leading male actors, each of them had popular appeal and each of them reflects the five recurrent values that we see in one form or another in virtually all cowboy movies. These values are inherent in American culture and they lie at the very heart of any explanation of why America invaded Iraq.

CHAPTER 4

....

VIOLENCE IN AMERICA:
INHERITED FROM COWBOY CULTURE

....

"Violence breeds violence and repression breeds retaliation. Only a cleansing of our whole society can remove this sickness from our souls."

—SENATOR ROBERT F. KENNEDY

Richard Slotkin, in Gunfighter Nation (1992), explained how the myths of the frontiersman and the cowboy have sanctioned local and national gun violence in America today. It is an ideology produced for us by mass-culture industries, and is exploited and kept alive by corporate and political elites. 1. Using violence as an accepted and legitimate means of resolving conflict was one reason why the White House chose to invade Iraq. George Bush had a choice. The United Nations was involved in a continuing series of weapons inspections in Iraq, looking for any trace of weapons of mass destruction, and had dealt with every disclosure with firmness of purpose. The USA could have continued to rely on the excellent and very accurate work being done by the UN inspectors. Saddam's nuclear program from the 1980's and 1990's had been dismantled by UN inspectors, as had his chemical and biological weapons programs.

John Prados, as part of his excellent analysis in Hoodwinked, said:

"There was no threat to the homeland of the United States, nor indeed any immediate threat from actual weapons of mass destruction. Many of the other charges were demonstrably false. The rest were ambiguous. None was anything the CIA and others had not known about for a long time. All could have been resolved by a process of international inspection to which Iraq had already agreed." 2.

The United Nations and the United States had Iraq under control, and severely limited in its ability to project power, at the time of the invasion in March of 2003. But violence as a solution to problems is an ingrained part of American culture, and George Bush, the cowboy president, chose violence over any peaceful resolution to the problem of what to do about Iraq. Violence is an endemic part of American culture, bequeathed by the cowboy culture of years gone by, and shamelessly embraced by George W. Bush's America.

The United States today suffers far more violent deaths than any other modern, industrialized country in the world. This is primarily due to the widespread presence of firearms, according to a report released by the National Research Council and the Institute of Medicine, two of the leading health research institutions in America. The US averages over 6 violent deaths per 100,000 in population each year. The only modern industrial nation that comes even close to that number is Finland, at 2 per 100,000 each year. Homicide is the second leading cause of death among adolescents in America, and most of these homicides involve guns. The United States has the highest rate of private firearm ownership in the world, being home to over one-third of all the privately-owned firearms world-wide. 3. According to the National Crime Victimization Survey, in 2011 alone, 467,321 people were victims of a crime involving the use of a firearm. The risk of death by homicide is twenty times higher in the US, than any other country of comparable GNP. Since 1968 more Americans have died from gun violence than from every war in U.S. history. 4.

One would think that the many deaths of children would resonate in America, but it doesn't. On December 14, 2012 Adam Lanza walked into Sandy Hook Elementary School and killed 20 students and 6 adults, before killing himself. He had previously shot his mother dead at home. He walked into a kinder-garten class and mercilessly gunned down 15 kids aged 5 and 6 years old. The National Rifle Association (NRA) reacted by stating that if the teachers were all armed, they could have fought back against Lanza. Imagine a school system where all teachers were issued loaded Colt .45's with their curriculum outlines, and fought pitched gun battles with armed students on a regular basis, like high noon in Tombstone.

At Virginia Tech University, a Korean student killed 32 students and staff and injured 23 before killing himself. At Columbine High School in Colorado, 2 shooters killed 15 and injured 24, before committing suicide. On Sunday morning, August 28, 2014 at 1 am, a shooter walked into a nightclub in Miami and opened fire, randomly shooting 37 young people. Five of the victims were girls aged 11-17. In Spring, Texas on July 9, 2014, Ronald Haskell walked into a home looking for his ex-wife and killed 4 young children and 2 adults, execution-style, lying them on the floor and shooting them in the back of the head. In Minnesota, James Ruppert shot dead his mother, his brother, his brother's wife, and their 8 young children. In October of 2015 a gunman murdered 9 students and teachers in Oregon before being shot by police.

Most other countries would be horrified at such carnage, but in America it is routine. Recently Canada suffered two deaths of soldiers who were murdered by ISIS sympathizers. There was an outpouring of both grief and consternation right across the country. One news commentator from the US observed this reaction across Canada to the 2 murders and said, by comparison, "In America we call this Wednesday."

There have been 69 mass shootings in the United States since 1982. The two most common venues for these mass murders have been either in schools or at workplaces. In the Washington navy yard recently, a shooter walked in and shot dead 13 fellow workers. In Minneapolis at Accent Signage Systems a fired worker returned with his gun and killed 6 of his fellow workers, including his supervisor and the owner of the company. In the summer of 2014 at a

UPS facility a disgruntled worker who had been fired shot his 2 supervisors to death and then killed himself.

South Carolina authorities on Wednesday, September 24, 2014 released a dash-cam video showing Highway Patrol officer Sean Groubert asking motorist Levar Jones to get his driver's license out of his car. Groubert then shot him in the hip as he reached into his car for the license. "Sir, why was I shot?" Mr. Jones could be heard saying.

On September 23, 2014 outside New Orleans, a 14 year old male, Cameron Tillman, unarmed and in no way a threat to anyone, was shot and killed by police for entering an abandoned house with three friends. That was harsh punishment for a B & E into an empty building. In Ferguson, Missouri 19 year old Michael Brown was shot and killed by a police officer. The policeman fired 11 shots at the unarmed Brown, who had his hands up and was surrendering when he was shot. The policeman was exonerated of any criminal charges. In Sanford, Florida George Zimmerman shot and killed an unarmed 17 year old, Trayvon Martin, claiming self-defense. The 30 year old Zimmerman, a mature male, was much larger than the slim teenage boy Treyvon Martin, and Zimmerman had a gun, but he was found not guilty. The carnage that has become a day-to-day experience in America leaves those in other countries astounded at the callous disregard Americans seem to show for their children or for life in general.

During the Christmas season in December of 2014 you could read about;

1. Two police officers in New York City who were murdered while sitting in their patrol cars. The perpetrator, before committing suicide, had talked of getting revenge for the deaths of unarmed blacks at the hands of white police officers.

2. Yet another teenager was shot dead by a police officer in St. Louis, Missouri.

3. Three people were injured, including two critically, in a Chicago train station when a gunman randomly opened fire.

4. A nine year old girl killed her gun instructor with an Uzi machine gun.

5. A man handling a plastic toy gun in a Walmart store while Christmas shopping was shot and killed by a SWAT team.

6. In an article titled <u>Americans Love Getting Guns for Christmas</u>, we could read of gun sales increasing by 4% as 175,000 Americans applied for new gun permits during the Christmas holidays. The article was followed by dozens of comments reflecting the joy of various Americans, from pre-teens to older adults, when they received guns as Christmas presents. Most Christians regard Christmas as being a time of peace and love, but in America it's a time to re-arm, and acquire a whole new arsenal of weapons.

The number of gun deaths did not diminish after Christmas. In early 2015 in northern Idaho at the local Walmart, a two year old boy took his mother's hand-gun from her purse while he was sitting in a shopping cart, shot her and killed her. A five year old boy took out his parents' handgun and shot and killed his infant brother as he sat in his crib. A 9 year old Girl Guide in Indianapolis was shot while delivering Girl Guide cookies. **5.**

Many try to understand the root cause of this gun mania in the United States. No other modern industrial nation has even a fraction of the gun deaths or a small percentage of the gun ownership, that there is in the USA. Coincidentally, no other modern industrial nation has a cowboy culture like that in the USA, as a significant part of its history. Cowboy culture, cowboy movies and their influence on American culture give a clear understanding of why guns and gun violence are not just tolerated but accepted as part of the American psyche. In cowboy movies, most people carry a gun, and many use gun violence to solve their problems. In every instance where the protagonists or the antagonists have a choice, they choose violence over other, more peaceful alternatives to dispute resolution.

In the cowboy movie <u>Open Range</u> (2002), Boss (Robert Duvall) and Charlie (Kevin Costner) are "free-grazers", cattlemen who roam the open prairie with their herd of cows. The first act of violence occurs off-camera when Mose, their powerful but child-like cowhand, goes to town for supplies. He gets into a fight with three men who work for the evil Baxter, the biggest rancher in the area. Mose defends himself courageously until the town Marshal, in the employ of Baxter, comes up behind him and cracks him on the head with his gun. Boss and Charlie go to town to find Mose and they become involved in a verbal confrontation with Baxter and Marshal Poole as they attempt to get Mose out of jail. Baxter finally issues an ultimatum, telling Boss under the threat of violence to take his cows and get out of Harmon County, and never come back.

At that point Charlie and Boss have a choice. They could leave in search of greener pastures, or they could choose violence and stay. They choose violence, stay in the Harmonville area and assault four of Baxter's men who are spying on their herd. They surprise the four men as they sit around a campfire. Boss asks which man has a sore back from fighting with Mose, and when the man is identified, Boss smashes him in the testicles with the stock of his rifle. He asks another man a question and when the man smiles, Boss turns his rifle into a baseball bat and smashes the man in the stomach, doubling him over. When he asks them to remove their pants and one man refuses, Boss hits him in the ear with the butt of his rifle and says, "Now listen outa your good ear." They break the men's rifles, run off their horses and then humiliate them by making them strip to their long-johns and lie in the dirt. Charlie is going to shoot them as they lie defenseless on the ground, but Boss stops him.

As they are attacking these four men in the woods, Baxter's other gangsters are attacking Mose and the 16 year old Button back at their camp. They shoot Mose in the head and kill him, they kill Charlie's dog, and they shoot Button, giving him a severe skull fracture, and almost killing him. At this point Boss and Charlie again have a choice, and again they choose violence. Boss wants to stay there on the prairie and wait for Baxter's men to come back so he can "kill them all". Charlie is more practical and wants to get a doctor for Button. Rather than riding on, or calling on the Federal Marshal, they ride into Harmonville, deposit Button at the Doctor's office, and then go into town and challenge Baxter and his men to a gunfight. While waiting for the fight to happen, Boss and Charlie go to the saloon. It is Baxter's saloon and they are refused service, so Charlie hits the barkeep in the face with a beer glass, and then blows out the mirror behind the bar with a shotgun blast. An interesting conversation ensues between Charlie and a local freight hauler. As they talk about how the town has deteriorated under Baxter's evil influence, Charlie says they could do something about it. When the man complains that they are freighters, not gunmen, Charlie says, "You're men, ain't ya? You might not know this, but there're some things worse than dying". The violence continues throughout the movie, leading up to the final bloody shoot-out, and Charlie's philosophical take on fighting violence with violence in defense of freedom reiterates a common theme in America.

The final shoot-out has been labelled the best gunfight in the history of cowboy movies by many film critics. In one ironic scene from that gunfight, one of Baxter's men is wounded and crawling away from the fight. Charlie catches up to the man and stands over him, ready to execute him, when Boss runs up to him and says "don't do it!" Charlie replies, "You said we were going to kill them all, Boss, and I aim to do just that" to which Boss states, "I said kill them, but not murder them." Charlie's response? "Splittin' hairs, ain't you, Boss?" The movie ends with a bloody slaughter in which all of Baxter's men are killed, and then at the climax, Boss kills Baxter as he lies bleeding in the Marshal's office. At every point when Boss and Charlie have a choice, they choose violence. At one point in the movie Boss makes fun of the option to just leave Harmonville behind, saying there's a fight coming and we're not going to "tuck tail and run" from a fight. Mose is killed, and the adolescent Button almost dies in the closing gunfight, Charlie and Boss are both shot and could have been killed, Baxter and his evil gang are killed, because violence is not just the last resort but the only resort when confronting evil. At one point Sue, Charlie's love interest, says "We could wire for the Federal Marshal" but that idea is quickly dismissed by Charlie and Boss as they push the plot inevitably to its violent and bloody conclusion.

Charlie and Boss in this film are symbols of the traditional cowboy character, and are the epitome of what it means to be an American. They work in relative isolation, and are individualistic, self-reliant, hard-working and heroic. These cultural values include gun violence, and this value has carried forward to the America we see today.

In the movie <u>Unforgiven</u> Clint Eastwood is our protagonist, Will Muny. A former desperado, he has changed his way of life for his wife, to become a hard-working farmer. His wife has died and left him with two young children, a boy of about 10 years of age and a girl who is about 6. Muny is given a chance to become a bounty hunter, and kill two cowboys for half of a $1000 reward. He leaves his two young children alone and defenseless in their isolated cabin, to go off and kill for money. He chooses violence over his duty to care for his children. After killing the two cowboys, and getting his reward, he discovers that his friend Ned has been tortured and killed by the evil town sheriff, Little Bill. Ned's dead body is standing up on display in front of the saloon. Despite the fact that his children are waiting alone at home for him, probably terrified, Muny goes into town and confronts a saloon full of armed drunks. He kills the saloon owner, and a number of others who try to fight back, and then shoots Little Bill. As he leaves the saloon he yells out that he will kill everyone in the town if they take a shot at him. Then he rides home to his children. What if he himself had been killed, and never made it back to his children? At each opportunity Will Muny chooses violence, and in the process puts his young children in serious danger, while causing the deaths of the two young cowboys, his friend Ned, the sheriff Little Bill and several other characters.

In the cowboy movie <u>Tombstone</u>, the screen explodes with violence in the opening scene, when seventeen members of the vicious "Cowboy" gang assault a smaller group of Mexican policemen at a wedding. Outnumbered and out-gunned, the policemen are slaughtered, the bridegroom is killed and the bride is taken into the church and raped by four Cowboys. The violence culminates when Johnny Ringo murders the priest while the other Cowboys take part in the wedding feast. This explosion of violence is but a precursor to what comes later. At every point in the plot when a choice is to be made, that choice is to use violence to solve problems. Wyatt assaults a young man when the man mistreats his horse, then Wyatt assaults Johnny Tyler in order to chase him out of the Oriental, and get a share of the gambling revenue in that bar. After repeatedly slapping Tyler, Earp says, "Are you going to do something, or just stand there and bleed?" Violence gives the Earps their start in Tombstone, when Wyatt secures a quarter interest in the Oriental after dispatching Tyler. Right after that violent scene, two friends of Doc Holliday's (both named Jack) are involved in a shoot-out in the saloon and kill a man over a game of poker, demonstrating the casual indifference to gun violence. Even when the towns-people are enjoying a theatrical performance, they have to be constantly shoot-ing their guns into the ceiling, or at objects on the stage. Very quickly after that performance a confrontation between Johnny Ringo and Doc Holliday in the saloon almost explodes into violence.

In an incident of unnecessary violence, the town Marshal Fred White is shot and killed by Curly Bill Brocious, who is drunk and stoned on opium. It is suggested by Wyatt that White ignore Curly Bill, who is shooting his pistol at the moon, but White chooses instead to confront him, and violence ensues. After Curley Bill is arrested by Wyatt, the Cowboys and Earps have their first head-on confrontation and this leads directly to the shoot-out at the O.K Corral. At the infamous shoot-out at the O.K. Corral Earp and his brothers, with Doc Holliday, go to confront the Clantons and the McLaurys, who are guilty of committing a misdemeanor. It is suggested by Wyatt that these men are drunk, and in the noonday sun will soon want to go and sleep off their alcoholic haze. But the option of just leaving them to sweat it out in the hot sun is quickly dismissed, and the Earps and Holliday go down to the corral and confront them, creating a violent and historic gunfight that could have easily been avoided. This gunfight in turn leads to Virgil Earp being bushwhacked and crippled for life, and Morgan Earp being gunned down and killed. In this wave of violence, one cowboy attacks the Earp wives with a shotgun in their home at night, and another fires a shotgun intro the home of the mayor and his wife.

At this point in the story Wyatt could have left with his brother Virgil for California. Both the Clanton/McLowry families and the Earp family have lost family members in the violence, and Wyatt could have called a truce right there and the violence may have ended. Instead we have the "Wyatt Earp Revenge Ride", in which Earp as Marshal takes his small posse and murders 27 members of the Cowboy gang. It began at the railway station, when Stilwell and Ike Clanton attempt to bushwhack the Earps. Wyatt kills Stilwell, then clubs Clanton over the head and rakes his spurs across Clanton's face. Earp then goes in search of vengeance. Earp is a Marshal, and entrusted with upholding the law. Rather than arrest any of these men, and take them in for trial, he takes the law into his own hands. He has a choice, and he chooses violence, and bloodshed splashes across the screen once again, just as it does in America today. The final bloody shootout between Doc and Ringo is but an exclamation mark on a continuing series of violent conflicts throughout this cowboy movie.

In the cowboy movie Butch Cassidy and the Sundance Kid there are several choices that ultimately led to violent conclusions. The movie opens with Sundance almost killing someone over a game of cards, a scenario that is shown repeatedly in cowboy movies. Shortly after that Butch gets into a knife fight over who should lead the Hole in the Wall gang. E.L. Harriman owns the Union Pacific Railway, and when he gets frustrated at Butch and Sundance constantly robbing his trains, he hires a "dream team" of marshals and trackers. But instead of charging them with bringing the outlaws to justice, and a trial in a court of law, he hired his posse for the sole purpose of killing Butch and Sundance, violence being his preferred solution. Later on in the movie, Butch and Sundance are in Bolivia and decide to go straight, getting a job guarding payroll shipments. Their boss is shot off his horse and killed by Bolivian bandits. Butch and Sundance trade the payroll for their lives and escape while the 6 bandits divide their ill-gotten loot. Butch and Sundance have a choice at this time, whether to ride into town and report the death of their boss and the loss of the payroll, or to attack the bandits and try to get the money back. They choose violence, and kill all 6 bandits. At the end of the movie, the Bolivian army have Butch and Sundance surrounded, and could have arrested them and charged them with their crimes. Instead the army blasts them into eternity, creating yet another bloody ending to a cowboy movie. In every instance where characters in the film have a choice, they choose violence over any other option.

Django Unchained, the latest cowboy movie to receive critical acclaim, was directed by Quentin Tarantino and thus involved a constant barrage of violent imagery. Much of the violence revolved around the theme of slavery, with the most horrific scene coming when one of the slaves, a runaway, was fed to a pack of hungry dogs. Equally repulsive was the scene in which two Mandingo fighters ended their bout when Calvin Candie handed the winner a hammer and instructed him to kill the loser with it. The explosion of gun violence at the end of the movie bordered on the absurd, but in many ways was a parody of the violent scenes at the end of Open Range, Butch Cassidy, Unforgiven and Tombstone. Just as horrible acts of gun violence appear in newspaper headlines almost on a daily basis in America today, so too does violence splash across the screens of cowboy movies.

With the onslaught of gun violence in America, President Barack Obama has tried repeatedly to have legislation pushed through Congress that would limit the purchase of automatic weapons, and prevent individuals who had a criminal record or had psychological issues from purchasing lethal weapons. The National Rifle Association, with multi-millions of dollars in donations to lobby congress, has won the support of Republicans, who have repeatedly shot down any legislation dealing with gun control. NRA members and Republicans want more guns, not less, so that the carnage in America's schools and homes, and in American workplaces, can continue unabated. On January 5, 2016 Obama unilaterally adopted legislation that would tighten background checks before weapons could be purchased. This would seem to be a logical although very limited approach to the gun epidemic in America, but Republicans and right-wing pundits roared their devilish protests over the simple process of keeping guns out of the hands of criminals and those who are mentally handicapped. Recourse to bloody mayhem seems to be a staunch Republican ideal.

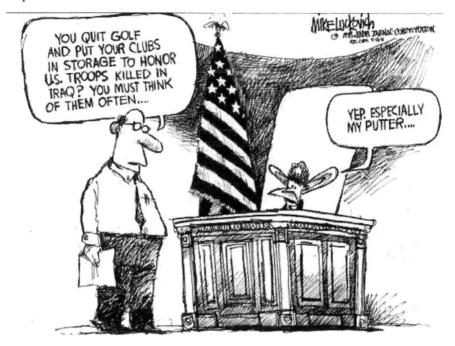

In a study done by the FBI, it was reported that mass killings in the USA have increased significantly in the past 6 years. The violence continues because it is an endemic part of American culture, a relic held over from the days of the cowboys. Just as in the cowboy movies, Americans pull out their guns when confronted with a crisis, and children die when they do. Bush pulled out his guns in Iraq, and innocent Iraqi children died by the tens of thousands. The cowboy president couldn't resist the call to violence, and so we saw Iraqi women and children being pulled out of the rubble, blood-soaked and bewildered, bodies torn apart by American war technology, and so many around the world wondering why this behemoth of a nation would bring such terror and bloodshed to a country that had never in any way threatened America. In Michael Moore's Academy Award-winning film Fahrenheit 9/11, we see live footage of Iraqi mothers holding up the dead bodies of their young children, crying and shouting into the video camera "WHY?" Other imagery included innocent civilians horribly burned by napalm, and young children killed by American bombs, their bodies horribly ripped apart. Between the 2003 invasion and 2011, 1,200,000 Iraqis died as a result of the violence created by America's illegal and much-condemned war, including 210,000 innocent civilians.

George Bush and his mercenary army destroyed the infrastructure of Iraq, murdered its citizens, and brought this country to its knees, and his stated motive was nothing more than a series of lies and mendacious prevarications. In January of 2005, well after it had been proven decisively that Saddam had no weapons of mass destruction, and was not sponsoring terrorism, Bill Frist, the Republican Senate majority leader, supported an embattled George Bush and justified the invasion of Iraq by saying, "Dangerous weapons proliferation must be stopped. Terrorist organizations must be destroyed." It was as if Frist was living in a time warp, totally oblivious to what was really happening in Iraq. The invasion had in fact increased the terrorist threat, as we see in Iraq today, and in San Bernardino, Paris and Brussels, and it accelerated the pro-liferation of dangerous weapons. Frist was lying to the American public in a most blatant and obvious way, just as Bush and Cheney used deception and fabrication to pave the road into Iraq. Cheney continued the mendacious com-ments when he reacted to the Senate torture report by defending his criminal behavior as being somehow "justified". His hubris rang falsely, containing not a trace of human dignity, as he dragged his nation's integrity through the muck and-mire of the still-seething war in Iraq.

"The greatest purveyor of violence in the world today… is my own nation," observed Reverend Martin Luther King Jr., in a comment that was made many years before Iraq, but could have been made today. **6.**

Shakespeare, in <u>Julius Caesar</u>, paralleled these comments when he eloquently described the bright facade of this fundamentalist Bush regime in his play about another "super power", the Roman Empire:

"And let us bathe our hands in blood up to the elbows, and besmear our swords. Then we walk forth, even to the market place, and waving our red weapons o'er our heads, let's all cry 'peace, freedom and liberty!'"

Over 4500 US soldiers have died and many more lay broken and disabled in America's underfunded military hospitals. Wally Lamb in his novel <u>We Are Water</u> framed the plight of the disabled in an incident in which a soldier in a military hospital with a head wound suffered in Iraq was being shown flash cards by a therapist. He was shown a picture of a banana, but couldn't find the word to describe what it was. Tears rolled down his cheeks as he said, "I know what it is…I've seen one before….but I can't remember what they are called."

Tens of thousands of American soldiers injured in Iraq or Afghanistan are suffering in military hospitals, and not being given the care that they deserve, a national scandal. George Bush had to drastically cut spending at military hospitals, while also cutting programs for the disadvantaged in American society, so that he could provide a $350 billion dollar tax cut ((May, 2003) for the very rich, "my people" he was fond of telling them.

William Blum in his book Killing Hope wrote about the first Gulf War. He said:

"While many nations have a terrible record in modern times of dealing out great suffering face-to-face with their victims, Americans have made it a point to keep at a distance while inflicting some of the greatest horrors of the age: atomic bombs on the people of Japan; carpet bombing Korea back to the stone age; engulfing the Vietnamese in napalm and deadly pesticides; providing three decades of Latin American dictators with the tools and methods of torture, then turning their eyes away, closing their ears to the screams, and denying everything…and now, dropping 177 million pounds of bombs on the people of Iraq in the most concentrated onslaught in the history of the world." 7.

Add to that the drone attacks in the Middle East, on various targets both legitimate and otherwise, and you have a full resume of long-distance murderous violence.

Historian Arno Mayer made this observation about the world after 1947:

"America has been the chief perpetrator of 'pre-emptive' state terror and innumerable other 'rogue' actions, always in the name of democracy, liberty and justice." 8.

Two common themes run through America's interventions in other nations. The first is that America claims it is defending human rights for civilians, although the interventions always leave behind massive collateral civilian damage. The second is that America claims it is acting in defense of freedom and democracy, but in many cases it is defending autocratic dictatorships that are controlled by pro-US elites.

Violence has become an American calling card, just as it was in the Old West. Rarely does a day go by that gun violence isn't used against family members, co-workers or fellow students. Rarely does a day goes by that America's military isn't taking violent action against another defenseless country somewhere in the world. In a nation with far more guns than in any other industrial democracy, the violent code from the "Old West" has been assimilated and it provided the impetus for the invasion of Iraq.

CHAPTER 5

GOOD VS. EVIL: THE BUSH MENTALITY

"Those who make war often think they make war in God's service, when really they are violating all of His laws."

— JOHN ADAMS U.S. PRESIDENT

In one speech, George Bush said, "My administration has a job to do and we're going to do it. We will rid the world of these evil-doers." In Winston-Salem, North Carolina on January 30, 2002 Bush said, "You know you've heard me talk about this probably but I really truly view this as a conflict between good and evil. And there really isn't much middle ground, like none. The people we fight are evil people". In an interview with Rich Lowry for the National Review in 2006, Bush said, "A lot of people in America see this as a confrontation between good and evil, including me." Glenn Greenwald in A Tragic Legacy said, "Extreme nationalism (of George Bush) is manifested as a belief that one's own country is intrinsically good and anyone who opposes it is pure evil". **1.**

A Los Angeles Times editorial in early 2007 stated:

"The 9/11 attacks reinforced the White House's penchant for viewing the world in binary terms, and Bush's 'with us or against us' mantra fit the moment. On issue after issue, from tax cuts to Iraq, this administration has portrayed opponents as beyond the pale, while its own positions are crucial to the defense of Western civilization". **2.**

By repeatedly referring to 'evil' and 'evil-doers', Bush was establishing a good guy/bad guy paradigm, thus re-enforcing the mind-set employed by the American military when the invasion of Iraq was launched. As Bush used phrases like "evil-doers" and "good guys/bad guys" to try and quieten critics of his increasingly unpopular war, his defensive stance re-enforced that western paradigm that often stands as an excuse for violence. His response to criticism of his war was slightly less obnoxious than Cheney's, who when told by a reporter that the majority of Americans did not support his war, offensively responded "So?" There was a man with absolutely no respect whatsoever for democratic values, with total contempt for the media and its role in society, and for no regard for the opinions of the people who elected him.

Establishing the framework of good guy/bad guy is a key part of cowboy movies, because it sets the stage for the violence that follows. Any statistics about innocent civilians being slaughtered in Iraq, or of torture being used on detainees, gets buried in the "good guy/bad guy" rhetoric. Ex-CIA agent Phillip Giraldi wrote about going to a Christmas party where most of the guests were CIA, and when the conversation turned to the morality of drone attacks in Pakistan, he over-heard from three different people, "We're the good guys. They're the bad guys." This euphemism has become the go-to excuse for Americans, to justify any violation of international law. Giraldi said:

"It's hard to be a good guy when we are killing American citizens without a trial, wiping out entire wedding parties. I admit that I was once on that page myself, but no longer, having seen America's good name trashed and transformed into what we once referred to as 'the evil empire'. That description may or may not have fit the Soviet Union in the 1980's, but it certainly fits us today."

Elizabeth Goitein is a director of the <u>Liberty and National Security Program</u> at New York University's School of Law. She spoke at length about the good guy/bad guy rhetoric, and had some interesting observations. She said:

"Bad guy is the term parents use to describe criminals to their four year olds, on the premise that young children lack the capacity for any more nuanced understanding. The term is symptomatic of the attitude that Americans should not ask, or seek to understand, the motivations of those who wish to attack us. The 'bad guy vs. good guy' frame of reference also precludes an objective assessment of America's own conduct in the war on terror. If terrorists are "bad guys," further inquiry is unnecessary. The caricature of "bad guy" versus "good guy" does our country a great disservice. It prevents us from understanding our enemies, a necessity in this unconventional war of ideologies...and it gives us false license to act against America's own stated values in the struggle." **3.**

Donald Trump would do well to heed the words of Goitein and Giraldi as he trumpets the failed values of torture and walls. Nazi Germany and Soviet Russia could give Trump good advice about pursuing increased torture regimes, and about building walls. It is only because he is so ignorant of history that Trump fails to see the striking analogy between his major campaign proposals and the actions of Adolph Hitler and Joseph Stalin.

Before Iraq, American public opinion was decidedly against torture of detainees. With the good guy/bad guy rhetoric firmly in place, Americans now have less of a problem with torture, seeing it as a necessary evil. George Bush obviously had a more simplified approach to the concepts identified by Goistein, having been inculcated with the cowboy philosophy from the Old West that the world is made up of good guys and bad guys.

In the opening scene from the movie <u>Tombstone</u> Curley Bill and his gang thought nothing of gunning down a group of Mexican policemen. He laughs afterwards, and said "looks like we win!" as if it was some kind of a game or sporting activity. It is reminiscent of a child-like George Bush, dressed in an airman's outfit reminiscent of The Village People, landing dramatically on the deck of an aircraft carrier anchored off the coast of San Diego and declaring, "In the battle of Iraq the United States and our allies have prevailed." No comment about the massive collateral damage in Iraq, no reference to the complete destruction of Iraq's infrastructure, and no comment about the many blatant lies that supposedly justified this illegal war.

In a paraphrase of Curley Bill's "looks like we win" comment, Bush continued by saying, "You have shown the world the skill and the might of the American armed forces". Where is the pride in destroying an enemy that was incapable of defending itself, an enemy that is $1/10^{th}$ the size of America, with less than $1/10^{th}$ the GNP and a vastly inferior military, never mind gloating "the United States and our allies have prevailed", as if there was any doubt at all as to the outcome? How could any nation take pride in the death and destruction brought down upon the innocent civilians of Bagdad by those video-game missiles labelled "shock and awe", when the Iraqi military was a well-known shambles? In any analysis of this attack, the word "bully" is difficult to avoid. The behemoth that is the US army, with its menacing, technologically-futuristic weapons and over-powering air attack, assaulted the small, defenseless nation of Iraq, which for the most part didn't even fight back...and Bush says,

"The United States and its allies have prevailed"? You prevail when you are in a tough fight, have the odds stacked against you, but manage to grind out a difficult victory. You don't "prevail" when you have the richest, most powerful and most technologically advanced army in human history, beating up a military as pitifully weak as was Iraq's. Bush's war against Iraq was a heavy-weight battle, but there was only one heavyweight in the fight, and he was scrapping against a veritable flyweight in Saddam Hussein and his pathetic army. It was no surprise when Saddam's army quit the battlefield less than two weeks after the fighting began.

This aggressive, bloodthirsty and totally unmitigated assault on a defenseless nation cast America very much in the role of the bad guy. Americans don't like to see themselves as the aggressors, asserting that they only fight as a last resort, like Charley and Boss in <u>Open Range</u>, when their backs are to the wall. America held off entering World War I until 1917, over three long years after it started, and didn't enter World War II until Pearl Harbor in 1941, two full years after the conflict began. But in this war America was very much the aggressor.

Writers and directors of cowboy movies deliberately manipulate the plot in the films so that we get a very clear picture of which characters are the good guys and which ones are the bad guys. Early cowboy movies even went so far as to have the good guys wear white hats, while all the bad guys wore black hats. Gene Autry and Roy Rogers always wore white hats. In every movie they starred in, and in most cowboy movies, the plot and the characterizations were manipulated to help justify the outburst of violence and the deaths that came later on.

In the cowboy movie <u>Open Range</u> we are treated in the opening scenes to a group of three men, Boss, Charlie and Mose and their 16 year old adopted cowhand, Button, and they are interacting like a family. They play cards with each other, joke with each other, help each other at work, and genuinely care for one another. Boss and Charlie take a paternal interest in young Button, upbraiding him in a fatherly way for cheating at cards, and chastising him for not keeping his feet clean. Charlie has a beautiful little white dog called Tig, and we see Mose playing with the dog constantly, causing Charlie later on to say, "He was more Mose's dog than he was mine." Mose tells Button he needs to respect men like Charlie and Boss, setting them up as role models. Mose is quite a big man, and when he tells Button, "Every man has to pull his own weight", Button replied, "But your weight is twice as much as mine", demonstrating the jovial, good-humoured relationship between the men. When Boss goes off looking for some runaway horses after a storm and returns with all the missing horses running in a herd in front of him, Mose says to Charlie and Button, "that Boss sure can cowboy", to which Charlie replies, "Yeah, they broke the mold when they made him." When Mose is late getting back from town with the supplies, Boss says, "You don't suppose he got into a poker game?" and Charlie immediately replies "He wouldn't gamble your money, Boss", reaffirming the inherent goodness of his colleague. There is so much mutual respect and admiration between these four that we can't help but see them in their little family grouping as the good guys. The director has in fact manipulated these opening scenes for precisely this purpose, so that the audience can see with stunning clarity that these guys are the good guys.

The first violence in the movie involves a three versus one fight, in which Mose is the victim. The Marshal cracks Mose over the head with his gun, from behind, and then while Mose is unconscious on the floor, Baxter's men kicked him repeatedly. Charlie later on says, "Looks like they put the boots to him after he was down" and the Marshal merely smirks and says, "Does it?"

Baxter demonstrates that he has the town Marshal in his back pocket, and we know for certain which characters are the bad guys. When Butler, one of Baxter's gun hands, kills Mose and shoots Button, then shoots and kills their little dog, Tig, it just clarifies who the audience is supposed to hate. Butler says to Charlie as the movie approaches its bloody conclusion, "and I enjoyed doing it too", proving just how evil he is. Charlie puts a bullet in his head and the audience feels that the violence is totally acceptable because of the "good guy/bad guy" dialectic that has been created. They are the bad guys, and when they are all killed by the good guys, it is called a happy ending. In many ways the killing of Baxter is analogous to the recent assassination of Osama Bin Laden by the American military. Bin Laden could easily have been brought to the United States, interrogated and prosecuted for his crimes, just as Baxter could have been arrested and charged for his many crimes. This is called "due process", one of the fundamental caveats of justice and international law going back to the Magna Carta. Don't good guys follow the law? One of the most important principles of Nuremburg was the concept of universality, the idea being that the law should be applied equally to all, including Osama bin Laden.

In the same way that Osama bin Laden was portrayed as the penultimate bad guy, thus justifying his assassination, so too are Baxter and his men so vividly portrayed as the bad guys, creating a scenario just like in Pakistan in which murder is totally justified. The violence becomes a normal part of cowboy life and not in any way an aberration.

In the conclusion to this violence a group of seven townspeople are seen in the background behind the town chasing one of Baxter's hoodlums. When he falls down, they all stand over him and shoot him repeatedly, getting a laugh from the audience for this cold-blooded execution. The audience of course is rooting for the underdogs. Charlie and Boss are fighting against overwhelming odds, and it is heart-warming to finally see the good citizens of Harmonville take sides in support of the good guys. It is only because we had been inculcated with the idea of "good guys/bad guys" that we look upon this cold-blooded murder as being comical. Charlie and Boss even joke about Baxter's death when Boss says, "There's a saloon back there just had its owner die". The death of Baxter has been translated into a joke, and a business proposition. No attempt is made to arrest anyone, or to involve the law in any way, because good guys know who the bad guys are and they recognize what needs to be done. Just as George Bush recognized Saddam as the bad guy and knew what needed to be done in Iraq, so too do Charlie and Boss recognize who the bad guys are in Harmonville, and they know what needs to be done.

The movie <u>Tombstone</u> is a virtual caricature of the good guys/bad guys dialectic. In the opening scene, the outlaw gangsters that call themselves "The Cowboys" ride into a small Mexican village where one of the local policemen is getting married. Curley Bill Brocious is the leader of the gang, and he says to the bridegroom, "Y'all killed two Cowboys." The Mexican is defiant and the Cowboy gang kills all of the policemen in the wedding party. After the Mexican police are all killed, the bridegroom is humiliated and then murdered, and then four of the Cowboy gangsters drag the young bride back into the church and rape her. While the Cowboys are taking part in the wedding feast, laughing and joking about the cold-blooded murders they had just committed, the priest who had performed the wedding ceremony comes over to them and incriminates them in Spanish with a passage from the Bible. Johnny Ringo shoots the priest in the head, kills him instantly, and gets a cruel laugh out of Curley Bill for this cold-blooded murder. At the end of this opening scene we have a very definite idea of who the bad guys are, and that sets the stage for the final bloodbath, often referred to as "Wyatt Earp's Revenge Ride".

Who are the good guys in this movie? We meet the three Earp brothers, Wyatt, Morgan and Virgil, with their three beautiful brides, as they stand together as a family, and look at their reflection in a store window. The three handsome men are all dressed in formal black suits, and the three wives are gorgeous, dressed in beautiful long dresses. All of the Cowboy gangsters are dressed in dirty work clothes, they are never seen with a woman, and it is never mentioned that they have wives or girlfriends. This further lends credence to the "good guys/bad guys" frame of reference. Towards the end of the movie, Wyatt goes on what is called his "revenge ride", and, acting as Marshal, he murders twenty-seven cowboys. The audience sees no problem with any of these cold-blooded murders, because they see it all within the framework of a "good guys/bad guys" paradigm. The bad guys shoot Wyatt's brother Morgan and kill him. Their method is cowardly, shooting him through a window, at night, and then running away. Virgil is bushwhacked in the same cowardly way, shot at night, during a thunderstorm, by bad guys who are hiding in the shadows. Doc Holliday, ambiguously one of the good guys, would never do that. He challenges Johnny Ringo to a gunfight face to face and kills him in a sport he calls "playing for blood". This movie reiterates the good guy/bad guy theme throughout, so that the extreme violence is acceptable and even normal. This norm translates readily into modern American culture.

In the movie Unforgiven the good guys/bad guys theme is somewhat ambiguous, because Clint in his portrayal of William Muny had been a hard-drinking, vicious thug in his early years. However, he has reformed, due to the influence of the woman he loved. He is seen at his wife's grave and our sympathy goes to him immediately, for he has two motherless young children to care for. Then we see two cowboys in a whorehouse, drunk, and one of the prostitutes laughs at one of the cowboys for having a "small pecker". The cowboy calls his buddy in from the room next door to hold the girl down, while he slashes her face with a large hunting knife. He cuts her badly, and leaves her scarred for life, unable to earn a living at her chosen profession. Little Bill (Gene Hackman) is the sheriff and he arrives to mediate. He sees the situation as one in which the owner of the whorehouse has suffered a business loss and must be compensated. So he orders the two cowboys to bring five horses into town in the spring and give them to the pimp. His consequence gives no consideration to the girl who had her face cut and deformed. It is left to the other prostitutes to raise enough money to put a bounty of $1000 on the heads of the two cowboys who cut her. We know now that Little Bill and the two cowboys are the bad guys, so when they are shot and killed the audience cringes, but feels that the violence is justified. William Muny kills Little Bill as he is lying on the floor, wounded and defenseless, but again this is justified because Little Bill is a "bad guy". Little Bill treats the cut-up prostitute with disdain, he humiliates and tortures poor English Bob before running him out of town, he beats William Muny to a pulp, when Muny is sick and can't defend himself. Finally, he tortures and kills Ned, then puts the dead body up on display in front of the saloon. The murder of Little Bill is totally justified because of his characterization as a "bad guy".

In the movie <u>Django Unchained</u> the slave-owners are the bad guys, and we learn this very early in the movie when Django and a number of other slaves are being marched while shackled together in chains. We see a slave being eaten by dogs, we see a slave being hit in the head and killed with a hammer, and we see a slave, Django's wife Broomhilda, locked while naked in a metal, coffin-like box under the hot sun. We see slaves being horsewhipped and otherwise treated like animals and when the good guy, rescued slave Django, launches his vendetta of terror by killing everyone in the Candie mansion, the audience is not repulsed and instead feels that this violence is totally justified. Dr. Schultz is also a "good guy" although he kills "bad guys" for money. Schultz befriends Django, treats him like a human being, and finally sacrifices his life to save Django and his wife Broomhilda.

George Bush identified Muslim Iraqis as "evil-doers", and the personification of evil, with reference to his invasion of the helpless little nation of Iraq, and by doing this he was first and foremost trying to legitimize the eventual deaths of 210,000 innocent civilians. More than that, he was trying to frame the conflict within the parameters of traditional cowboy morality. By using good guy/ bad guy rhetoric, and by calling the Muslim Iraqi people "evil-doers", he was both justifying his illegal war and giving the American public, and the lapdog, sycophantic media, a frame of reference within which they could slot the various horrors committed by the American army in Iraq. Bush invoked the "good guy/bad guy" mantra of the traditional cowboy movie, and by doing so seemingly absolved America of its many horrendous war crimes.

Sgt. Geoffrey Millard served in Tikrit with the 42nd infantry division. He testified in an investigation about how his unit had established a traffic control point and an 18 year old American soldier was manning a 50-caliber machine gun on top of an armored Humvee. As a car drove towards them, the 18-year-old soldier hit the butterfly trigger and put 200 rounds into the vehicle, killing a mother and father, their 4 year old son and their 3 year old daughter, as they were headed out on a shopping trip. When Millard reported this incident to the commanding general, a colonel in the room turned to the full division staff and said, "If these fucking Hajis learned to drive this shit wouldn't happen", demonstrating a level of compassion that was truly morbid. 4. Haji is a derogatory, racist term similar to the racist epithets "skinny" or "raghead" or "sand nigger" used constantly by American soldiers to demean the people they were terrorizing. In Vietnam, the local people were referred to as "gooks" or "slants" or "dinks", all of these terms racist slurs that degrade the humanity of those being murdered. With so many years of practice calling black people "niggers" in their own country, and calling Spanish-Americans "spics" or "greasers", the American soldiers had no problem castigating Iraqis with racist slurs. It was the good guy/bad guy framework that allowed this colonel to respond with such open disdain to these violent and unnecessary civilian deaths. One hundred and fifteen American soldiers in Iraq committed suicide in just one year, 2007, many because they couldn't live with themselves after such horrible incidents of carnage. Sixty-nine American soldiers were charged with killing Iraqi civilians, only a small fraction of those who should have been charged. One soldier, after returning from Iraq in 2005, said, "I don't feel young now. I think I am old in my heart."

The good guy/bad guy rhetoric only worked in America, where the press made no effort to pursue investigative journalism and instead put a corrupted version of patriotism ahead of journalistic integrity. The rest of the world watched in horror as the US became the merciless, brutal invader, attacking a defenseless nation that had never at any time been a threat to America. The image of heavily-armed American soldiers going into someone's home and murdering the unarmed and defenseless family members there should haunt any American with a conscience. On November 19, 2005, after an IED killed Lance Corporal Miguel Terrazas, members of his unit killed fifteen unarmed Iraqis, including eleven women and children. Marines killed all of the occupants of a passing vehicle, then entered nearby houses and killed everyone there, men, women and children. 5. On December 31, 2007 the Marines dropped the charge of unpremeditated murder against Staff Sergeant Frank Wuterich for failing to stop the squad under his command while a massacre of innocent civilians was occurring in Haditha. His defense was that he was following rules of engagement established by superior officers, a defense that didn't benefit Nazi defendants at Nuremburg. **6.**

The very worst part of this "good guy/bad guy" framework and the "evildoers" characterization by Bush, was how it empowered American soldiers to commit some of the most horrific atrocities imaginable at Abu Ghraib prison in Iraq, clarifying for everyone with stunning clarity who the bad guys were.

Antonio Tuguba, a major-general in the U.S. army, described photographic and video evidence at Abu Ghraib prison in which a teenage Iraqi boy was screaming in terror while a US army translator sodomized him. A female US soldier was watching and taking pictures as this rape was taking place. Several photographs showed American soldiers raping Iraqi female prisoners while they were locked in their jail cells, trapped and totally defenseless. There were photos of American interrogators sexually assaulting prisoners with truncheons, a wire and a phosphorescent tube. Pictures showed Iraqi prisoners being sodomized by American soldiers with metal batons. In a report in the New York Times on January 5, 2005, soldiers were pictured urinating on prisoners, they were punching prisoners' open wounds, they were pouring phosphoric acid on detainees, and they were tying ropes to their penises and dragging them across the floor. Guards regularly threw rocks at detainees when they were defenseless and sleeping in their cells, and detainees were shot and killed for very minor violations of the rules. A number of prisoners were killed and dragged away in the middle of the night, without ever having been recorded as having been there. Juan Frederick kept a video diary and in it he said about a dead Iraqi prisoner; "The next day the medics came in and put his dead body on a stretcher, put a fake IV in his arm and took him away. He was never processed, never had a number."

Prisoners were completely immobilized, for days at a time, with chains, and kept without food or water for 48 hours or more. Sleep deprivation involved strobe lights and loud rock music blared into cells repeatedly so that some prisoners didn't sleep for 5 days. Male prisoners were made to wear women's underwear, and female US soldiers were brought into the cells of naked male prisoners to humiliate them with crude comments about their genitals. Abuse of the Q'uran (Koran-Islam's Holy Bible) happened repeatedly. One military police officer said to a soldier acting as a prison guard, "I don't give a fuck what you do to him. Just don't kill him."

Soldiers threw poisonous snakes into the prisoners' cells at night, in the dark, and several prisoners died of snake bite. American soldiers forced the detainees to crawl naked on the floor while they rode them like donkeys. We need to keep reminding ourselves that, according to Bush, these were the good guys. President-elect Barrack Obama promised to release these photographs and videos once he was installed in the White House in 2009. However, after viewing the photographs and videos himself, he found that they were so incredibly disgusting that he could not in good conscience expose the American public to such reprehensible and perverted behavior. He was also concerned that the outrage in Iraq, if the evidence of gross debauchery was made public, would expose American soldiers to even worse danger than what they already faced. 7.

Major-General Taguba, for revealing this disgraceful behavior to the public, was subsequently fired from his job by Secretary of Defense Donald Rumsfeld for "not being part of the team". In response to that vengeful act, Taguba said,

"There is no doubt as to whether the current administration has committed war crimes. The only question remaining to be answered is whether they will be held to account." **8.**

On May 26, 2004, Al Gore stated, "In Iraq what happened at that prison is not the result of random acts of a few bad apples. It was the natural consequence of the Bush Administration policy." Gore called Bush the most dishonest president since Richard Nixon. Senator Lindsay Graham said, "The American public needs to understand that we're talking about rape and murder here."

Pierre Krahenbuhl from the <u>International Committee of the Red Cross</u> said;

"Acts of prisoner abuse were not isolated acts but were part of a pattern, a broad system tantamount to torture…there were clearly instances of degrading and inhumane treatment".

The Bush government tried repeatedly to put the blame on those lower down in the echelon, but evidence quickly surfaced that the orders involving torture and the degradation of prisoners of war, in direct violation of the Geneva Conventions, came from the offices of Dick Cheney, Condoleezza Rice and Donald Rumsfeld. It became pretty obvious then, that Bush was fully knowledgeable about what was happening at Abu Ghraib, and on April 11, 2008 Bush admitted that he had approved the torture protocols.

On June 26, 2003, as the United States was enacting a torture portfolio approved by George Bush, he would state in public:

"Today, on the United Nations International Day in Support of Victims of Torture, the United States declares its strong solidarity with torture victims across the world. Torture anywhere is an affront to human dignity everywhere. We are committed to building a world where human rights are respected and protected by the rule of law. Freedom from torture is an inalienable human right. <u>The Convention against Torture and Other Cruel, Inhuman or Degrading Treatment</u>, ratified by the United States and more than 130 countries since 1984, forbids governments from deliberately inflicting severe physical or mental pain or suffering on those within their custody or control." **9.**

On another occasion Bush said:

"I want to be absolutely clear with our people and the world: The United States does not torture. It's against our laws, and it's against our values. I have not authorized it, and I will not authorize it." **10.**

Within months of President Bush's June 2003 speech, Manadel al-Jamadi died in CIA custody at Abu Ghraib Prison. He had been taken from his home by US Navy Seals who "repeatedly kicked, punched and struck" him with weapons, according to an official investigation. He was later hooded and made to kneel with his trousers around his ankles while he was without underwear, and was doused with water while a CIA officer interrogated him. He was then taken to Abu Ghraib Prison still naked from the waist down, with his legs shackled and his head covered with a plastic sack and his wrists so tightly bound behind his back with plastic flexi-cuffs that a guard reportedly had "trouble cutting them off." He died under interrogation. In one of the photos of that abuse at Abu Ghraib prison, US guards can be seen smiling and giving the "thumbs up" sign over al-Jamadi's dead body. An autopsy concluded that his death was caused by "blunt force injuries of the torso complicated by compromised respiration," and that he was a victim of homicide, while in custody. However, no one has been found criminally responsible for the killing of Manadel al-Jamadi. **11.**

On December 10th, 2014 the Senate Report on Torture was finally released, and in his reaction to that report, Cheney stated quite firmly that Bush was well aware of all aspects of the torture portfolio. Cheney angrily retorted about the report, "The program was authorized. The agency did not want to proceed without authorization." **12.** Bush's executive order of February 7, 2002 authorized the torture program that existed at Guantanamo, and the horrors at Abu Ghraib, thus contradicting his public statements about torture.

George Bush deliberately misled the American people so many times, without being held accountable by the media in the United States, and his prevarications became those of a man who felt he could say anything that came to mind, with complete confidence that he would be supported by the media. Under his watch, the United States changed from a nation that condemned torture and forbade its use, to a nation that practiced torture routinely, and seemed to relish in it. That is a sad indictment of a nation that at one time took pride in its world-wide stance against torture.

Rush Limbaugh, one of Bush's most ardent supporters, had this to say about the torture being done at Abu Ghraib:

"Someone has to provide a little levity here. This is not as serious as everyone is making it out to be....this is a pure media-generated story. This is no different than what happens at the Skull and Bones initiation...I'm talking about people having a good time...you ever heard of emotional release? You ever heard of the need to blow some steam off?" **13.**

Like so many Republican apologists, including George W. Bush, Dick Cheney, Mitt Romney, Sean Hannity, Rudy Giuliani and Newt Gingrich, Limbaugh has never at any time done anything in his personal life to suggest character traits implying courage or bravery. Like Limbaugh, they all dodged the draft for Vietnam, letting others risk their lives rather than stepping up and fighting for their country. These cowards bellow from the highest roof-top about warrior character traits, and the need for young Americans to risk their lives in Iraq, yet turned yellow and turtled when it was their turn to serve in Vietnam. Their hypocrisy knew no bounds as they spent virtually their entire careers pushing paper in Washington, creating the conditions under which thousands of young American soldiers wasted their lives needlessly. Now Republicans looking to secure the 2016 presidential nomination are vigorously competing against one another to see who would adopt a torture protocol even more horrible and more brutal than the gross violations of international law that Bush and Cheney perpetrated.

Taking a historical look at torture, there was during World War Two an elite American Army unit stationed at Fort Hunt that was charged with interrogating Nazi prisoners of war. An article in the Washington Post in 2007 reported about their reunion, the first time they had gathered together since WW2 ended in 1945. These proud soldiers expressed regret about the tremendous gap between the way they conducted interrogations during that war and the harsh measures used today in questioning terrorist suspects.

"Back then, they and their commanders wrestled with the morality of bugging prisoners' cells with listening devices. They felt bad about censoring letters. They took prisoners out for steak dinners to soften them up. They played games with them. Several of the veterans, all men in their 80's and 90's, denounced the controversial techniques used at Guantanamo and at Abu

Ghraib. The interrogators had standards that remain a source of pride and honor. 'During the many interrogations, I never laid hands on anyone,' said George Frenkel, 87, of Kensington. 'We extracted information in a battle of wits. I'm proud to say I never compromised my humanity.'" **14.** This is a statement that neither Bush nor Cheney could ever make.

Outside Abu Ghraib prison, what happened in Fallujah established with certainty just who the bad guys were in this fiasco of a war. Americans deliberately targeted Fallujah General Hospital in its initial assault on that city in order to mute the statistics about civilian casualties that made America look so bad. In yet another attempt at fabrication, George Bush had said:

"With new tactics and precision weapons, we can achieve military objectives without direct violence against civilians." **15.**

Donald Rumsfeld also spoke about US military bombing raids, saying "the targeting capabilities….the care that goes into it…the humanity that goes into it."

210,000 innocent civilians were killed in Iraq, and Bush described it as "without direct violence against civilians"? Tomahawk missiles and 2000 lb. penetrator bombs were dropped on Bagdad in a vain attempt to assassinate senior Iraqi officials. Although not a single senior Iraqi official was killed by these bombs, a 100% failure rate, Iraqi civilians died by the thousands. Many of the weapons used in the bombing of Bagdad were cluster bombs, which opened up after landing and ejected hundreds of mini-bombs across densely-populated neighborhoods. Over 90,000 of these mini-bombs failed to explode, and were left to lie in playgrounds and schoolyards as unexploded landmines. Thousands of children were killed or maimed by these lethal weapons. The Pollyanna storyline about precision bombing emanating from the White House was in stark contrast to the civilian bloodbath taking place in Iraq. Soldiers testified about little girls with their faces disfigured, their noses blown off, husbands carrying their dead wives, sobbing, families having to hold 5 funerals in one day, because of the "care" and the "humanity" that went into Rumsfeld's bombing raids.

The assault on Fallujah was correctly labeled a "massacre", with many of the victims being women and children. As previously mentioned, Fallujah General Hospital was responsible for collecting and publicizing information about civilian deaths in Fallujah, so the hospital became a primary target of American bombing raids. Interesting war strategy, and in direct violation of the Geneva conventions, which state that "fixed establishments and mobile medical units of the Medical Service may in no circumstances be attacked, but at all times shall be respected." Dr. Sami al-Jumaili described how US war planes bombed the Central Health Center, killing 35 patients and 24 staff. His report was confirmed by the BBC. **16.** Dr. Eiman al-Ani reported that the entire health center had collapsed on the patients after American bombing raids. **17.** This was not a surprise, for the al-Nouman Hospital and the Yarmouk Hospital in Bagdad were both deliberately targeted in the initial assault on Bagdad in March of 2003. In addition to the Falluja General Hospital being targeted in the 2004 massacre, the Nazzal Emergency Hospital in Falluja, operated by a Saudi Arabian charity, was reduced to rubble by American bombing raids. In yet another open violation of international humanitarian law, the US military denied the Iraqi Red Cross access to Falluja, to care for the many wounded. The entire medical staff at one hospital was tied up by American soldiers, while innocent civilians, women and children, were bleeding to death in the streets with no one available to help them.

American military atrocities also included attacks on the media that reported their bad deeds. A prominent reporter from Al-Jazeera TV had his home bombed after his unfavorable coverage of the Falluja massacre in 2004. Al-Jazeera had previously given the coordinates of its Bagdad headquarters to the American military so that no mistakes could be made. The U.S. military used those coordinates to bomb Al-Jazeera headquarters on April 8, 2003, in retaliation for Al-Jazeera reporting the many civilian deaths in Iraq that military reports in the U.S. neglected to mention. This was no surprise, for the Al-Jazeera headquarters in Kabul had previously been targeted, on Nov. 12, 2001, after it reported similar civilian atrocities in Afghanistan. **18.** Sajah Hassan, a photojournalist representing Al-Jazeera was arrested for no reason other than doing his job and was forced to stand naked for 11 hours before being released without charge.

Jean Ziegler of the UN Special Rapporteur on the Right to Food accused US troops in Falluja of "breaching international law by depriving civilians of food and water, using hunger and deprivation of water as a weapon of war against a civilian population" **19.**

After blockading the city and not allowing anyone to leave, neither women nor children, the US military brought down all of its destructive power on that city, completely leveling it and causing a certified massacre because of all the civilian deaths. One American soldier wrote in lipstick on a bathroom window in one of the destroyed homes, "Fuck Iraq, and every Iraqi in it!", thus clarifying for everyone with absolute certainty just who the bad guys were. **20.**

In the spring of 2003 Joshua Key was sent to Ramadi as part of the 43rd Combat Engineer Company. He and his squad were sent out to assist American soldiers who were supposedly under attack by more than one hundred armed Iraqis. When they arrived at the scene, there were four dead Iraqi civilians and three American soldiers, but no armed Iraqi insurgents anywhere. One soldier screamed out, "We fucking lost it, we just fucking lost it". The three soldiers had used their M-16's to decapitate the four Iraqis, completely severing their heads. As the one soldier sat there in a state of psychological breakdown, the other two were laughing and kicking the Iraqi heads around in their own twisted game of soccer. Key asked his sergeant later on if the incident had been reported and he was told quite vehemently to forget what he had seen. This was just one of a number of terrible atrocities that Key witnessed while serving in Iraq. **21.**

Key told in his book <u>A Deserter's Tale</u> of befriending a seven year old Iraqi girl when he was on guard duty at a hospital. The girl would run up to the fence and ask Key for food rations, called MRE, then take them back to her family. In return she brought him bread cooked fresh at home by her mother. The last time he saw her, after many visits, she ran up towards the fence, was about ten feet away and he heard a burst of automatic fire from an M-16 behind him, and watched the girl's head explode like a mushroom. One of his fellow soldiers had killed her, a shock that Key says stays with him to this day. **22.**

In summarizing his exposure to so many gross atrocities in Iraq, Key said:

"The killing of the four Iraqi civilians, the games American soldiers played with their heads, the silence of my own military commanders...all combined to snap the last threads of belief I had in my country and what it was doing at war. I had always seen my fellow Americans as upholders of justice in the world, but now I had come face to face with the indecency of our actions in Iraq. I didn't know much about the Geneva Convention but I knew one thing: what I had witnessed was wrong....we were supposed to be stomping out terrorism,

PATRICK O'NEIL

bringing democracy, and acting as a force for good in the world. Instead we had become monsters in a residential neighborhood…I didn't have to be a lawyer to know that armies at war were not supposed to rape, plunder, loot or pillage. They were not supposed to harm civilians or mutilate the bodies of the dead. The American military had betrayed the values of my country. We had become a force for evil, and I could not escape the fact that I was part of the machine." 23.

After two tours of duty in Iraq, Joshua Key and his family moved to Canada to avoid another tour, thus earning the label "deserter". In the conclusion of his book, Key said, "I participated in hurting the people of Iraq and I paid a price for it. Ordinary Iraqis have paid very dearly for this war, and ordinary Americans are paying for it too, with their lives and with their souls. I will never apologize for deserting the American army. I deserted an injustice and leaving was the right thing to do. I owe one apology and one apology only, and that is to the people of Iraq." 24.

America's bad guy role has a historical precedent and was honored in Vietnam with such classic films as <u>Apocalypse Now</u>, <u>Platoon</u> and <u>Casualties of War</u>. The slaughter of 504 civilian peasants in My Lai by Lieutenant William Calley and his platoon saw these innocent victims machine gunned to death in their villages, with many young mothers and young girls raped before they were executed. In one scene reported by several soldiers, women were covering their babies with their bodies to protect them from being shot. American soldiers shot all the mothers, and then turned the mothers over so that they could shoot their babies in the head. An American helicopter crew tried to stop the carnage but were threatened by their fellow soldiers on the ground. They did manage to save a small number of villagers before departing. The deplorable true story of sexual violence in Vietnam depicted in <u>Casualties of War</u>, in which an American patrol kidnapped an 18 yr old Vietnamese girl and systematically raped her every night while moving through the jungle, is eerily reminiscent of what happened in Iraq, when four American soldiers scouted the home of a 15 year old Iraqi girl, then went back to her home that night, tied up her family, and then gang-raped her, while her family listened to her screams. The soldiers then executed everyone in the house, so that there would be no witnesses. The incident only came to light because one of the soldiers allowed his conscience to get the better of him and confessed. How many similar incidents were never reported?

The 'good' in the good guy-bad guy paradigm isn't the good that is referred to in the Christian Bible, not the traditional moral definition of good. It is simply what is "good" for America. For many evangelical Christians in America, this 'good' was sanctioned by God and existed in stark contrast to the evil of Islamic fundamentalists. In truth there was very little that was 'good' in the murderous assault on Iraq, and the good guy-bad guy paradigm, in Shakespeare's words, "jangled out of tune and harsh".

Reddit.com is an internet website that poses interesting questions and then publishes the most popular responses, as rated by its readers. One question asked by the website was, "Are we the good guys or the bad guys in Iraq?" A responder who called himself "Digital Caveman" had one of the most highly-rated responses.

"I used to think Americans were the good guys, but then I did a year in Iraq with the US Army. Seeing first-hand what we do to people in other countries completely changed my mind. I felt like the bad guy occupying someone else's country, blowing up kids with artillery, and just fucking shit up over there."

A response from perkyN405 was also ranked very high in audience approval.

"Good guys don't lie. Good guys don't torture. In the darkest period of the American Revolution, George Washington refused to use torture, a common interrogation tactic of that time. In WW2 the US refused to use torture. We even executed one Japanese war criminal after the war for waterboarding a single American. Bush shit all that down the drain....no, we are not the good guys."

George Bush called his book, written after his second term had expired, "Decision Points". Was one of his decisions to put raw aggression and civilian slaughter ahead of his Christianity? Was one of his decisions to indulge in repeated deceptions and fabrications designed to con the American people into supporting a war that was both illegal and totally unnecessary, ultimately causing the deaths of over 4500 American soldiers? Was one of his decisions to set aside "Thou shalt not kill" in favor of "Thou shalt enrich the military-industrial complex"? How much thought did he put into the decision to trade off 1,200,000 Iraqi lives for hundreds of billions of dollars in profits for his good friends at Halliburton, The Carlyle Group, General Dynamics, Blackwater and Exxon?

Political analyst Anatol Lieven commented that Americans had been "duped by a propaganda programme which for systematic mendacity has few parallels in peacetime democracies". **26.**

American soldiers were manipulated and deceived into fighting an illegal war in Iraq, and were summarily thrust into the role of the bad guy by a cowboy President whose lack of integrity and insouciant superficiality were an insult to their patriotism. Bush used good guy/bad guy rhetoric to manipulate his country into a war that was completely unnecessary, completely illegal and completely in violation of every good guy principle we see in America's cowboy movies.

CHAPTER 6

···

MANIPULATING AND ABUSING
INTERNATIONAL LAW

···

"Bush violated FISA because he wanted to violate the law in order to establish
the general principle that he was not bound by the law, to show that he
has the power to break the law, that he is more powerful than the law."

—GLENN GREENWALD

While rationalizing their war plans, both Britain and the United States cited various UN resolutions to justify the legality of their attack on Iraq. But international legal experts, including the International Commission of Jurists, the U.S.-based National Lawyers Guild, a group of thirty-one Canadian law professors, and the U.S.-based Lawyers Committee on Nuclear Policy have found this legal rationale to be untenable, and are of the view that the invasion was not supported by UN resolution and was therefore illegal. According to a detailed legal investigation conducted by an independent commission of inquiry set up by the government of the Netherlands headed by former Netherlands Supreme Court president Willibrord Davids, the 2003 invasion violated international law. In 2005 a German court ruled that the Iraq war was illegal under international law. 1.

The International Military Tribunal at Nuremburg held following World War II that the waging of a war of aggression is "essentially an evil thing...to initiate a war of aggression...is not only an international crime; it is the supreme international crime, differing only from other war crimes in that it contains within itself the accumulated evil of the whole".

Benjamin B. Ferencz is a retired law professor and was one of the chief prosecutors for the United States at the military trials of German officials following

World War II. In an interview given on August 25, 2006, Ferencz stated that not only Saddam Hussein should be tried for war crimes, but also George W. Bush because the Iraq war had been begun by the U.S. without the permission of the UN Security Council. Ferencz wrote the foreword for Michael Haas's book, George W. Bush, War Criminal? The Bush Administration's Liability for 269 War Crimes. Ferencz elaborated as follows:

"A prima facie case can be made that the United States is guilty of the supreme crime against humanity, that being an illegal war of aggression against a sovereign nation. The UN charter clearly prohibits the use of armed force except in very limited conditions of self-defense. The U.S. invasion of Iraq was unlawful." **2.**

Anne-Marie Slaughter, dean of the Woodrow Wilson School at Princeton and president of the American Society of International Law concluded that "the invasion was both illegal and illegitimate". **3.**

In March 2003, Elizabeth Wilmshurst, then deputy legal adviser to the British Foreign Office, resigned in protest of Britain's decision to invade without Security Council authorization. Wilmshurst stated that the English Attorney General Lord Goldsmith also believed the war was illegal, but didn't speak his mind because of fears he would lose his job. She held a similar view of Jack Straw, British Foreign Secretary, who like Goldsmith 'changed his mind' and endorsed the war at the last minute, presumably under pressure from Tony Blair. In 2010, Britain's deputy prime minister Nick Clegg, during prime minister's questions in Parliament, asserted that the Iraq war was illegal. **4.**

In many cowboy movies, we see the law being treated with disdain, in much the same way that Bush treated the UN and international law with disdain when he invaded Iraq. The invasion of Iraq not only violated the UN charter, but also contradicted the Nuremburg protocols agreed to after World War 2, and it contradicted the American Constitution. The invasion violated several aspects of the Geneva Conventions, as George Bush flaunted international law. The United States has often proclaimed its support for the rule of law in international affairs, and has at times been very insistent that other nations and world leaders be held to account. Just recently, American government officials were calling Assad, the leader of Syria, a "war criminal", a designation that fits George Bush and Dick Cheney far more comfortably. Before invading Iraq, Bush officials warned Saddam's generals about being charged with war crimes.

Americans have consistently denied the concept of universality, a most crucial aspect of international law, by making these accusations while at the same time refusing to accept the application of international law when it came to the behavior of Bush, Cheney and the other war criminals in the Bush regime.

This contempt for international law didn't begin with George Bush. As far back as 1963 President John F. Kennedy advisor Dean Acheson instructed the American Society of International Law that no legal issue arises when the United States responds to a challenge to its "power, position and prestige". **5.** In other words, America has free rein when it comes to the use of violence in international affairs. More recently, in May of 1997 William S. Cohen reported in regard to Bill Clinton's doctrine, that the United States is entitled to resort to unilateral force to ensure "uninhibited access to key markets, energy supplies and strategic resources". **6.**

More recently still was the total lack of any kind of uproar when Osama bin Laden was assassinated. America's long tradition of justice before the law, going back to the Magna Carta, took a direct hit with this violation of international law. In an on-line article on May 13, 2011 at ThinkProgress.org titled <u>International Law is Made by Powerful States</u>, commentator Matthew Yglesias remarked, "One of the main functions of the international institutional order is precisely to legitimate the use of deadly military force by western powers." Therein lies a total exemption from all aspects of international law, the theory being that America can bring force to bear on any small, defenseless country it chooses to bully, with no recourse to the Geneva Conventions, the Nuremburg protocols, the U.N. charter or even its own constitution. Like the cowboys in so many western movies, the United States was empowered by Acheson, Clinton and Yglegias to treat international law with disdain, and the Bush regime did just that in Iraq.

Being a cowboy by nature, George Bush had no problem showing his contempt for international law. He had seen this attitude replicated in so many cowboy movies, where the law was used and abused, that it became second nature to sweep aside the dictates of the UN, the Geneva conventions and the Nuremburg protocols. Right after 9/11 Bush adopted the façade of a testosterone-laden, muscle-bound cowboy by stating, "I don't care what the international lawyers say. We're going to kick some ass." **7.**

On January 25, 2002 Counsel to the President Alberto Gonzales issued a memorandum stating that the Geneva Conventions were "quaint" and "outmoded" and were therefore inapplicable to the United States. **8.** Jack Goldsmith, head of the Justice Department's Office of Legal Counsel, called the Gonzales memo "a conspiracy to commit a war crime." **9.** To George Bush it was a green light, and he used this cowboy mentality with enthusiasm.

In the cowboy movie <u>Tombstone</u> the law is a complete farce. The contempt for the law begins when "The Cowboys" execute the Mexican policemen in the opening scene. Violence directed towards policemen continues when Curley Bill shoots and kills the local Marshal, Fred White, and again when Virgil is shot and crippled, and when Morgan is killed. Both are working as police officers in Tombstone when they are attacked, demonstrating contempt for the law. This demeaning portrayal of the law continues with the Sheriff Behan characterization. Although a lawman, he is a close associate of the murdering Cowboys, even deputizing this notorious outlaw gang so that they can try to hunt down and kill Wyatt Earp and his deputies. At every turn in the plot, Behan is weak, cowardly and highly ineffective as an officer of the law. Earlier in the movie, when Curley Bill is having his opium-fueled meltdown, it is the obsequious Behan who is the coward and refuses to step in, instead coercing the much older Fred White into taking action, leading to White's death. When the shootout at the OK Corral takes place, the cowardly Behan is found hiding out in the building next to the corral. Only after the fighting has ended does Behan step in, saying to the Earp's and Doc Holliday, "Ok. You men are all under arrest." Wyatt Earp steps towards him and says with great contempt, "I don't think I'll let you arrest us today, Behan." Behan, intimidated by Earp, quickly backs down, thus fulfilling his role as the cowardly, ineffective Sheriff.

Later on in the movie, Wyatt Earp is sworn in as a US marshal, but is busy assassinating any Cowboy he can catch, all while wearing a badge. At the railway station he sees his brother Virgil off to California, and then kills the bushwhacker Stilwell. He accosts Ike Clanton and shows him his marshal's badge. He tells him to tell his friends; "See this badge? It says United States Marshal. Tell them the law is coming. Tell them I'm coming...and hell's coming with me!" He manages to murder twenty-seven Cowboys during his infamous ride, without once resorting to the criminal justice system. We even see him lynching two cowboys, both of whom had never been charged with a crime. Earp taking the law into his own hands is a defining characteristic of cowboy culture in Tombstone, and a defining characteristic of the Bush regime when it invaded Iraq. Portraying representatives of the law as being weak and cowardly parallels the Bush regime's portrayal of the UN, when it was referred to as a "debating club" and was called "irrelevant". The law means nothing to Earp or his followers other than a badge to authorize the coming executions, just as international law meant nothing to George W. Bush.

When the actor Fabian is killed by two Cowboys for defending Josie's honor, Billy resigns from Behan's posse, saying to Behan "I'm sorry sir- but we've got to have some law." The implication is that the Marshal and the Sheriff, together with the men who ride with them, are behaving like gangs of outlaws, and not like men who are appointed to uphold the law. Like George Bush they have no respect for the law, and no intention of enforcing it.

When Doc is lying in bed dying of TB, Wyatt puts his marshal's badge on Doc's chest, before he goes out to fight Ringo. Doc gets out of his sickbed, kills Ringo himself, and then sets the badge on Ringo's chest, saying his hypocrisy goes only so far. Throughout this movie, the law is held up to ridicule, and manipulated by those in power just to suit their specific goals. The law is obsequious, it is powerless and it is ultimately meaningless, paralleling the Bush regime's attitude towards international law.

In Open Range, Marshal Poole is working for the evil cattle baron Baxter, and has no intention of upholding the law with any sense of fairness. At one point Sue says, "You're a disgrace, Marshal Poole" and he replies, "I know it. That's just the way it is." In the final shoot-out Poole sides with Baxter and his gang, and at one point threatens to shoot the 16-year-old Button, who with a fractured skull is lying defenseless in the street, thus underlining for everyone the moral depravity of this lawman. Throughout the movie, Poole is portrayed as a blustering, obsequious puppet, and answers only to the dictates of the evil Baxter. Twice when Charlie indicates that he is willing to have a gunfight with Poole, the Marshal backs down, his cowardly character yet another indication of how disrespected officers of the law were in the Old West. At one point in the movie Open Range, Marshal Poole ends up in chains, locked in his own jail. Boss smacks him on the nose with his revolver, and then drugs him with chloroform, and in his incoherent state is a perfect metaphor for the law in this town. The law is a façade in Open Range, and is treated with disdain. When Sue suggests to Boss that "we could wire for the Federal Marshal", this idea is summarily dismissed because the alternative, a lawless, violent shoot-out, has far more appeal to two cowboys totally committed to cowboy culture. Says Boss in the café, "We've got a warrant filled out for them that killed the big fella (Mose)…and we aim to enforce it!!" and Charlie says to Sue later, "There's payment to be made to them that done this". Recourse to the law, or any legal resolution to this conflict, is discounted in favor of a violent and bloody confrontation, just as George Bush opted for a bloody assault on Iraq rather than a legal resolution through the UN. Irony reigns supreme when the last bloody shots in the final confrontation take place in Marshal Poole's office, the building that should have been a symbol of law and order. In the final analysis, Boss and Charlie simply are doing what needed to be done, well outside the parameters of legal recourse, in the same way that Bush by attacking Iraq was, in his own mind, doing what needed to be done. The big difference was that Baxter and Poole are far more of a threat to Boss and Charlie, than Iraq ever was to the USA.

In <u>Unforgiven</u>, Little Bill, played by Gene Hackman, represents the law. He is the Sheriff in the town of Big Whiskey, where most of the story takes place. His first action in the movie is to arbitrate the situation in which the prostitute is cut by the two cowboys. In most jurisdictions, one would think the Sheriff would arrest the two men for assault and have them appear before a judge. This consequence may have forestalled the violence that follows. However, Little Bill has his own rather peculiar approach to the law, and sees the conflict not as one in which the girl has been assaulted, but rather one in which the business owner (ie. the pimp) has lost equity in one of his business assets-the woman. Ignoring the serious physical damage done to the woman, and in the process ignoring the laws governing assault, Little Bill arbitrates by having the cowboys give five horses as compensation to the pimp. Because Little Bill, as a representative of the law, abrogates his responsibility towards the law, we have all of the violence and killing that ensues. Following that pattern, Little Bill deals with the bounty hunter English Bob in his own unique fashion as well, totally and violently outside the law, and when he first encounters Will Muny, Little Bill arbitrarily and severely beats him almost to death. There is no arrest, no charges before a judge, just the Sheriff beating a man who is sick and posing no threat to anyone. During the movie we see Little Bill trying to put a roof on his house. He fails miserably and during the first rainstorm he has to place buckets all around the floor to catch the rain coming through the roof. In this inconsequential sub-plot, we see the incompetence of this representative of the law and we see his colleagues treating his efforts with ridicule.

In the incident that immediately precedes his own violent death, Little Bill captures Ned, then tortures him and kills him, after which he hangs Ned's dead body outside the saloon. At no time do we see this officer of the law acting like a lawman. No arrests, no charges, no judge, no jury. Little Bill is judge, jury and executioner, and he makes a farce of the law. His brutal death at the end of the movie is again an image of the law lying dead, in disgrace, on the dirty floor of a saloon.

In Butch Cassidy and the Sundance Kid we see a town Marshal trying to rally the local town-folk into joining a posse to chase Butch, Sundance and the Hole in the Wall gang. The Marshal is held up to ridicule as the locals turned their attention instead to a bicycle salesman, and ignore his pleas to join his posse. While the Marshal is berating the townspeople, Butch and Sundance are sitting on the balcony of the local whorehouse enjoying a beer and watching the proceedings, thus showing their utter contempt for the law and for the Marshal. When Butch and Sundance are on the run, they hide out in the home of an officer of the law, who also happens to be their friend. They talk with him about alternatives to jail and suggest that they could join the army and go fight the Spanish. They ask for his help, as a friend, to absolve them in some way for their outlaw past. Before Butch and Sundance leave the Marshal's house, he asks them to please tie him to a chair, so that his neighbors won't suspect that they are friends. In a relationship that parallels the Behan/Cowboy relationship in Tombstone, we see again the outlaws being good, personal friends with the Marshal.

The lawmen who are part of the posse hired by E. L. Harriman to hunt down and kill Butch and Sundance have no compunction about taking part in a planned execution. They have no intention whatsoever of arresting Butch and Sundance and bringing them to trial. Although they are officers of the law, these bounty hunters are perfectly willing to take on the role of assassins and commit murder, if the price is right. Using officers of the law as paid assassins is yet another farcical treatment of the role of the lawman in traditional westerns. They play the role of the Navy Seals who went after Bin Laden in Pakistan. Later on in this movie, when Butch and Sundance rob their first bank in Bolivia, several local policemen chase them out of town. Butch and Sundance hide in some trees and shoot at the policemen, after which the police turn quickly and ride back to town, laughably obsequious and once again making policemen look like buffoons.

In today's world there is international law. There is the UN charter, there is the Geneva Conventions, and the World Court. George Bush asked the United Nations to support war with Iraq and the UN quite logically said no, because there was no basis for attacking Iraq. Bush ignored the wishes of the United Nations, violated Geneva Conventions and international law, and he and his regime would have been considered war criminals on a par with the Nazis of WWII, had the United States given the World Court any legitimacy at all. After World War Two ended, during the Nuremburg trials, Joachim von Ribbentrop was charged as a war criminal, and hanged, for being complicit in a pre-emptive strike against Norway. 10. The principle at Nuremburg was that "planning, preparation, initiation or waging of a war of aggression or a war in violation of international treaties, agreements or assurances, is a war crime." This principle became a prerequisite for judging war crimes. Does not the prerequisite at Nuremburg, and the repeated reference by American leaders to international law and war criminality, not also make Colin Powell and George Bush subject to prosecution as war criminals? Colin Powell went to the UN, representing George Bush, and produced totally fabricated stories as the basis for an invasion of Iraq, a country that was not even a remote threat to the United States. If the same standard of international law is to be applied consistently, as it was at Nuremburg, why weren't they, and the other White House war criminals, put on trial? The concept of universality, of the law being equally applicable to all, was a key concept of Nuremburg and was part of the foundation of international law agreed to by the United States following World War Two. The crime of aggression is "the supreme international crime" according to Robert Jackson, Associate Justice of the Supreme Court and U.S. chief prosecutor at the Nuremburg war crimes trials. He reiterated that the law applies equally to everyone, supporting the universality of international law. 11.

As with most bullies, the United States has abrogated its commitment to universality, and considers itself above the law. America was more than willing to send Colin Powell to the UN, to regurgitate the lies that Bush had unashamedly repeated over and over on American television. As soon as the UN Security Council was seen not to go along with Bush's adventure in catastrophe, the White House ignored all pretense of recognizing international law, and began plundering Iraq.

George H. W. Bush, who presided over Gulf War 1 in 1990-1991, was also faced, as his son was, with the legal decision of whether to invade Iraq and overthrow Saddam Hussein. After chasing Saddam out of Kuwait, and thoroughly defeating his army, Bush was encouraged on several fronts to continue on to Baghdad, but he declined to do that. In his memoirs he said:

"Trying to eliminate Saddam would have incurred incalculable human and political costs.......Going in and occupying Iraq, thus unilaterally exceeding the United Nations mandate, would have destroyed the precedent of international response to aggression that we hoped to establish. We had been self-consciously trying to set a pattern for handling aggression in the post-Cold War world. Had we gone this invasion route, the United States could conceivably still be an occupying power in a bitterly hostile land. It would have been a dramatically different-and perhaps barren-outcome." 12.

George Jr had no problem with exceeding the mandate of the United Nations, and 13 years after his invasion America continues to wage war in both Iraq and Syria, just as his father had predicted. George H. W. Bush recognized the legal parameters involved in invading Iraq and unseating Saddam Hussein, and he respected the principle of universality inherent in international law. George Bush Jr. recognized neither of these principles, because his values were still trapped within the mythology of the Old West and the legendary cowboys he grew up with. As with many recovering alcoholics, he had a difficult time leaving his childhood behind.

On April 21, 2003 George W. Bush said:

"The stakes are high, and the Iraqi people are looking- they're looking at America and saying, are we going to cut and run again?" 13.

This comment was a brutal critique of his father's decision not to invade Iraq in 1991 and overthrow Saddam Hussein, and it helped define a fractured relationship between father and son. This fracture was further revealed with George W's appointment of Donald Rumsfeld as Secretary of Defense. Rumsfeld had been a bitter enemy of George Bush Senior for many years, and had actively campaigned to keep Bush Senior off the Republican ticket in 1980 as Ronald Reagan's running mate. The discord between father and son was further revealed when Rumsfeld and Cheney became the most predominant power brokers in the White House, while close friends of George Senior, Brent Scowcroft and Colin Powell, were marginalized, with no voice in the Bush Junior administration. When asked why he didn't go to his father for advice on Iraq, Bush Junior stated, "You know, he is the wrong father to appeal to in terms of strength. There is a higher father I appeal to." **14.** Bob Strauss, U.S. ambassador to Moscow under Bush Senior, said of the differences between Bush Senior and Bush Junior; "Bush Senior finds it impossible to strut, and Bush Junior finds it impossible not to. That's the big difference between the two of them." 15.

According to author Craig Unger:

"What Bush Senior didn't say was that he knew at the deepest, most fundamental level that if George W. ever made it to the White House, he would be in way over his head." **16.**

George W. Bush's disrespect for the law was pervasive, paralleling his disrespect for his father. In an outrageous attack on legal parameters in his own country, on September 6, 2006 President Bush asked Congress to amend the War Crimes Act of 1996, to decriminalize certain acts retroactively. Criminal acts that Bush was admitting to, and trying to overturn, included disappearances, recourse to extrajudicial imprisonment, torture, transporting prisoners between countries and denying the International Red Cross access to prisoners.

The New York Times reported in 2005 that "Bush had ordered the National Security Agency (NSA) to eavesdrop on the electronic communications of Americans without obtaining the warrants required by relevant criminal law. This warrantless eavesdropping had been going on for four years and had targeted millions of Americans".

Yet another instance that highlights Bush's complete disdain for the law is the case of Canadian Maher Arar. He was seized at JFK airport on September 26, 2002 as he was travelling from Tunisia to Montreal, returning from a holiday. After Bush labelled him an enemy combatant, for absolutely no justifiable reason, he was denied legal counsel, prevented from seeking help from the Canadian embassy, and was flown to Syria. He was imprisoned and tortured for 13 months before it was determined that he had no connection whatsoever to terrorism. Arar was one of four Canadians who had no connection to terrorism, but were detained and tortured with no recourse to the criminal justice system. Kaled el-Masri was one of many innocent American citizens who suffered a similar fate. Stories abound of innocent civilians who were mentally handicapped, suffered from drug addictions and other serious psychological issues, or simply were Muslims traveling for business or pleasure and yet were railroaded by aggressive counterterrorism agents and ended up in prison with sentences of up to 30 years.

George Bush and Stephen Harper, Canada's ex-Prime Minister, should have listened to Winston Churchill's comments on this topic, when they were passing laws that attacked the very pillars of democracy:

"The power of the executive to cast a man into prison without formulating any charge known to the law, and particularly to deny him the judgement of his peers, is in the highest degree odious, and the foundation of all totalitarian governments, whether Nazi or Communist." **17.**

Reporters Without Borders in 2004 began listing countries according to the amount of press freedom that was tolerated by their respective governments. That first year under George Bush the United States was ranked 17th in the world. In 2005 America under the Bush regime dropped to 44th in the world, in terms of press freedom. By 2006, the Bush administration had allowed America's rating for press freedom to drop to 53rd place, alongside Botswana, Croatia and Tonga. **18.** When calculating the many violations of international law by the Bush regime, one need only look at America's world ranking in terms of press freedom to understand how these war criminals were able to violate international law with such impunity. What an embarrassing indictment for a nation that has in the past cherished and protected the democratic value of freedom of the press.

As a consequence of Bush's almost total disdain for the law, virtually the entire list of lawyers employed in the U.S. Department of Justice, including former Attorney General John Ashcroft, either resigned or threatened to resign in reaction to the overt law-breaking and complete disrespect for international law being perpetrated by the White House after 9/11. The consequences of this disdain for the law had more widespread implications when Washington criticized Malaysia for indefinite detention and torture of alleged terrorists in 2003. The Malaysian response was that they were simply following the policies and procedures of the American government at Guantanamo. Egypt, Zimbabwe and Sudan were also criticized for the same reason, torture of detainees, indefinite imprisonment without charges and no access to a lawyer. They too used Guantanamo as the rationale for the illegal detention and torture of suspected terrorists in their prisons, saying in effect to the Americans that 'we are just doing what you have been doing'.

Noam Chomsky wrote about his country's historical disrespect for international law. He said:

"International law, treaties and rules of world order are sternly imposed on others with much self-righteous posturing, but dismissed as irrelevant for the United States- a long-standing practice, driven to new depths by the Reagan and Bush II administrations." **19.**

The attitude of disrespect for international law shown by the entire Bush cabinet was underlined by Lord Bingham, former United Kingdom law lord, in November 2008 when he said:

"Particularly disturbing to proponents of the rule of law is the cynical lack of concern for international legality among some top officials in the Bush administration." **20.**

An intriguing story about international agreements and the rule of law followed Secretary of State Condoleezza Rice to Mexico in March of 2005, where she criticized the Mexicans for not following through on a treaty signed in the 1940's governing Mexican water being diverted to the United States. The Mexican authorities agreed to deal with the issue, then brought up the 51 Mexicans on death row in America, a situation that had been governed by the Vienna Convention on Consular Relations. The United States had proposed that convention in 1963 and had signed it in 1969. The convention basically states that when a person from a foreign country is charged with a capital crime, they have the right to consult with their embassy representatives as to their legal status and their legal alternatives, before facing trial. These 51 Mexicans were deprived of that right, in contravention of the Vienna Accord. When the World Court in The Hague ruled against the USA in this case, America simply announced it no longer supported the Vienna Accord and "withdrew" its commitment to that treaty. When asked to explain the obvious contradiction between that treaty and the water treaty, Rice stated, "We will continue to believe in the importance of consular notification, but international court jurisdiction has proven inappropriate for the United States." **21.** The ability of the United States to enforce its interpretations militarily no doubt played a role in Mexico's acquiescence to this double standard, a scenario that plays itself out all over the world as America absolves itself from all aspects of international law that interfere with its ability to dominate the globe, yet expects all other nations to follow international law explicitly.

Ramsey Clark is a former US Attorney General and an outspoken advocate of the point of view that the first Gulf war was also highly illegal. In his book The Fire This Time: US War Crimes in the Gulf he said that we should keep in mind "that the policy and practice of the American war had repeatedly violated the letter and the spirit of the United Nations Charter, the Hague Conventions, the Geneva Conventions, the Nuremburg Tribunal, the protocols of the International Committee of the Red Cross and the US constitution, amongst other cherished documents." 22.

On February 21-22, 1991 Russia intervened in the first Gulf War and was able to convince Iraq to withdraw completely from Kuwait. George Bush Sr. in turn guaranteed that the retreating Iraqi army would not be attacked. Yet as the Iraqis retreated to Basra, they were bombed and strafed and rocketed mercilessly. Mike Erlich of the Military Counseling Network spoke at the European Parliament hearings in March-April of 1991. He said:

"….thousands of Iraqi soldiers began walking toward the U.S. position unarmed, with their arms raised in an attempt to surrender. However, the orders to this unit were not to take any prisoners. The commander of the unit began the firing by shooting an anti-tank missile through one of the Iraqi soldiers. ….at that point, everyone in the unit began shooting. Quite simply, it was a slaughter." 23.

The British daily The Independent said, "It was sickening to witness a routed army being shot in the back." They further said that it turned the stomach to see the glee with which the Americans carried out the barrage. US forces fired on Iraqi soldiers after the Iraqis had raised white flags of surrender. American tanks had large plows pulled behind them, and as the tanks fired into the Iraqi soldiers in their trenches, the plows buried the Iraqis under huge mounds of sand, no matter that they were still alive, wounded or dead.

In Baghdad, American bombers hit a civilian air raid shelter one day after the Pentagon announced that all of Saddam's military weapons had been destroyed or rendered inoperative. Fifteen hundred Iraqi civilians were killed in that attack, the majority being women and children. Laurie Garrett, a medical writer for Newsday, viewed unedited video footage of that attack and said;

"They showed scenes of incredible carnage. Nearly all the bodies were charred into blackness; in some cases the heat had been so great whole limbs had been burned off. Among the corpses were babies and children, most of them so severely burned that their gender could not be determined. Rescue workers collapsed in grief, dropping corpses; some rescuers vomited from the stench of the still-smoldering bodies." **24.**

The Pentagon admitted after the war that "non-military facilities had been extensively targeted for political reasons", the thinking being that such attacks would encourage desperate citizens to rise up and overthrow Saddam.

In yet another egregious violation of international law, the United States chose to ignore the ruling of the World Court in regard to America's terrorist war in the 1980's against the tiny, defenseless country of Nicaragua, the second poorest country in Central America after Haiti. The United States was ordered by the World Court and the Security Council of the U.N.to cease its war crimes against Nicaragua and to pay reparations for the damage done. America chose to simply ignore the World Court, and the UN Security Council, one in a continuing series of incidents in which the United States chose not to follow the very dictates of international law that America helped to formulate after WW 2.

The United States signed the North American Free Trade Agreement with its good friend Canada twenty-five years ago, but has abrogated several aspects of that treaty since then. When the World Court ruled against the USA in those instances, the United States insulted its Canadian friends by simply refusing to recognize the jurisdiction of the World Court. One can hear the voice of Condi Rice in the background saying again that the rulings of the World Court in The Hague were "inappropriate" for the United States. Despite these egregious insults to the foundation of international law, Bush in his State of the Union address in 2007 could say with a straight face, "We are all held to the same standard, and called to serve the same good purposes." He was talking about universality, a concept that was dealt with quite thoroughly at Nuremburg, but which is no longer an American value.

The United States was very clear at the end of World War Two in regard to its desire to establish a set of moral principles upon which the world community could govern itself. The Nazi war crimes tribunal at Nuremburg was part of the foundation of a new world order based on international law. The UN charter, the Geneva conventions, international treaties and the World Court in The Hague all came to signify the validity of international law. But, just as in the cowboy movies, this basis of international law was treated with disdain and disrespect by the United States, when it came to its plundering of Iraq. George Bush remembered well from his youthful days watching cowboy movies that taking the law into your own hands, and ignoring or disrespecting the law, was consistent with cowboy values.

Violations of international law by the USA over the past 65 years are too numerous to detail here, but three are noteworthy. Iran has been virulently anti-American for many years now, and this sentiment was high-lighted when Iranian students attacked the American embassy in 1979, taking 52 people hostage and setting the stage for the Academy Award-winning movie Argo. One idea that was not explored in any detail in that movie was why the citizens of Iran harbored such hatred for America. As with the attacks on 9/11, this incident too was inappropriately labelled as "senseless violence". How many Americans were aware that the United States had deprived Iranians of their democracy in 1951, deposed their elected president Mossadegh and installed brutal dictator Shah Reza Pahlavi as their corrupt leader. He ruled under CIA sanction for over 25 years. 25.

For most of the 20th century Iran was pillaged by the West, first by Britain and then by the United States. These two empires did whatever was necessary to keep that cheap oil flowing, including murder, torture, illegal imprisonment, death squads, and imposing puppet tyrants while assaulting democratic values. In 1951 Mohammed Mossadegh was elected by an overwhelming majority in parliament to be Iran's Prime Minister. His first order of business was to nationalize Iran's oil industry, a move that enraged both the US and Britain, but was wildly popular in Iran. Shortly thereafter, John Foster Dulles, Secretary of State in the US, met with a group of top-level policy-makers in Washington and said,"This is how we get rid of that madman Mossadegh." 26. Mossadegh was a madman because he wanted Iranian oil to belong to Iranians, clearly an idea to be ridiculed. Dulles presented a plan drawn up by CIA operative Kermit Roosevelt to overthrow the elected leader of Iran. Roosevelt said later in his memoirs, "This was a grave decision to have made. It involved tremendous risk. Surely it deserved thorough examination, the closest consideration, somewhere at the very highest level. It had not received such thought at this meeting. In fact I was morally certain that almost half those present, if they had felt free, or had the courage to speak, would have opposed the undertaking." 27.

With the complicity of the British, America launched a ruthless and paralyzing economic blockade of Iran, freezing Iranian assets and bringing all of Iran's foreign trade and its entire economy to a standstill. Using over $19 million in bribe money to corrupt Iranian parliamentarians, army generals and other prominent Iranians, the CIA invoked every dirty trick in the book to undermine Mossadegh and drive him out of the country. Roosevelt then created a totally artificial campaign to encourage Iranians to accept the Shah as their leader, bribing thousands of Iranians (including many street criminals) to stage mock demonstrations pretending public support for the Shah to be installed as Iran's new leader. Once installed by the CIA, the Shah then appointed Fazlollah Zahedi as the new Prime Minister. Zahedi had been in prison for collaborating with the Nazis during World War Two. What followed for the next 26 years was a brutal military dictatorship, fully supported by the United States. Savak, the secret police in Iran who were trained by the CIA, routinely jailed, tortured and killed any Iranians who protested the dictatorial rule of the Shah. To ensure support for the Shah, the CIA then began paying regular, annual bribes to Iran's religious leaders, beginning in 1953 and continuing until 1977, so that they would encourage the populace not to revolt against this very unpopular despot. The ayatollahs and mullahs were rumored to have received up to $40,000,000 a year of U.S. taxpayer dollars in secret payments over these 24 years, and it was only when Jimmy Carter cancelled these payments in 1977 that the ayatollahs began fomenting revolution in Iran. Iranians had every reason to hate America when they attacked the American embassy.

Iraqis have harbored a similar grievance. In the 1960's, General Abd al-Karim Qasim deposed the Iraqi monarchy and took over as leader in Iraq. One of his first major decisions as leader was to get the Americans, British and French out of the Iraqi oil business, so that Iraq's oil could be for the benefit of the people of Iraq. This insult to the imperialistic Americans was not tolerated and the CIA got involved in ousting Qasim. This move led directly to the rise of the Baath Party and Saddam Hussein. Americans pretend at being supporters of democratic values worldwide, but this value is only applicable when it is consistent with America's goal of dominating global politics. **28.**

Even more abhorrent than the events in Iran and Iraq was America's attack on democratic values in Chile in 1973, again sponsored by the CIA. Salvador Allende was the democratically-elected president of Chile. Unfortunately for him, he proposed legislation that was not in the best interests of the American copper-mining companies, or the multinational corporation International Telephone and Telegraph. At the urging of these American corporations, the CIA helped organize a military take-over of that democratically-elected government. This take-over included the assassination of Allende, the deaths of tens of thousands of young Chileans who tried desperately to restore their country's fledgling democracy (including a number of young Americans also butchered by the Chilean military, under the direction of the CIA), and the installation of one of the world's bloodiest and most brutal military dictators, General Augusto Pinochet. He was later tried before the World Court in The Hague and convicted for "crimes against humanity" but died before suffering the consequences of his actions. **29.**

William Blum said in his book <u>Killing Hope</u>:

"They closed the country to outsiders for a week, while the tanks rolled and soldiers broke down doors. The stadiums rang with the sounds of execution, and the bodies piled up in the streets and floated in the river. Torture centers opened for business and 'subversive' books were thrown on bonfires...and the men in Washington opened up their chequebooks." **30.**

This vicious, unlawful American attack on democratic values was artfully and emotionally portrayed in the movie <u>Missing</u>, starring Sissy Spacek and Jack Lemon. Lemon's son in the movie played a young American who had gone to Chile to support Allende's democracy, but ended up being butchered by the goons that the CIA had turned loose. His story was loosely based on the real-life tragedy of Charlie Harmon, a young American living in Santiago. He made the mistake of talking informally with several CIA operatives whom he had met in a bar. They told him that they had come to Chile "to do a job". Harmon "disappeared" shortly after that conversation, and was never seen again. Ask the people in Chile about America's worldwide support for democratic values. Pinochet remained in power for over 20 years, with the support and assistance of the USA and the CIA. Corporate America was appreciative, although democracy definitely took a hit in Chile, as it did in Iran.

Americans often seem puzzled when they hear about how disliked they are around the globe, thinking that it is unfair and irrational. Americans often say that the hatred that they face is due to anti-American hatred for "our way of life, our freedoms". Bush has said that on several occasions in regard to Islamic hatred of America. Soldiers who fight in America's imperialistic wars overseas and put themselves in harm's way are often praised for defending "our way of life", by politicians who would never put themselves in harm's way. **31.**

Journalist James Fallows wrote in <u>Atlantic Monthly</u>:

"The soldiers, spies, academics and diplomats I have interviewed are unanimous in saying that 'They hate us for who we are' is dangerous claptrap." Fallows called it "lazily self-justifying and self-deluding". **32.**

Michael Scheuer , first chief of the CIA's bin Laden unit, said:

"Bin Laden has been precise in telling Americans the reasons he is waging war on us. None of the reasons have anything to do with our freedom, liberty, and democracy but have everything to do with U.S. policies and actions in the Muslim world." **33.**

In November 2004 the Pentagon confirmed this point of view, stating "Muslims do not 'hate our freedoms' but rather they hate our policies." **34.**

As early as February 27, 1993, after the first bombing of the World Trade Center, Islamic terrorists wrote a letter to the <u>New York Times</u> in which their concerns were laid out clearly and concisely. The first was that the U.S. should stop all military, economic and political aid to Israel. The second was that America should terminate diplomatic relations with Israel. The third was that the U.S. should not interfere with the interior affairs of any Middle Eastern country.

Americans have a very difficult time acknowledging that there is very good reason for the people in the Middle East, in Central and South America, in Asia and elsewhere to hate America. Violations of international law, interference in the politics and policies of other nations, and support for ruthless, violent dictatorships have built a foundation for hatred around the world.

Canadian citizen Omar Khadr, the first juvenile ever to be charged with a war crime, can testify to American disrespect for the law. He was arrested as a 'terrorist' when as a 15 year old boy he was trying to defend his village in Afghanistan against the invading American army. When he was finally arrested by the US military, he had two bullet wounds in his back, and had been brutally beaten, subsequently losing the vision in one eye as he was left with his eyeball hanging out on his cheekbone. After being threatened with immediate execution, he confessed to killing an American soldier. Jailed with adults in Guantanamo for 6 years without ever having charges laid against him, he was kept in solitary confinement and tortured repeatedly before finally being brought before a military commission. In January of 2008 the UN Special Representative for Children in Armed Conflict requested permission to attend the legal proceedings for Khadr but this permission was denied. This was not a surprise because the United Nations has been repeatedly denied access to all American-run military or CIA prisons. The UN for years has been trying to have child soldiers designated as victims of war, rather than enemy combatants, a designation the Americans have firmly rejected. Before a US military commission, Khadr was given the choice of pleading guilty and doing another 8 years behind bars, or pleading innocent, and spending the rest of his life at Guantanamo. This violates every international convention you can think of, including laws on the treatment of juveniles. How many countries living by the rule of law, with any sense at all of human rights or the treatment of children before the law, hand 15 year olds a life sentence, for any crime, let alone one based on a confession obtained through brutal torture? People who defend Khadr's continuing incarceration looked to his confession and his guilty plea as proof that he deserved his sentence, with no knowledge or understanding of how that confession, and his later guilty plea came about. 35.

America has flaunted international law, the protocols of Nuremburg and the Geneva conventions, and interfered brutally in the internal politics of sovereign nations for years. From Haiti to The Philippines to Panama to El Salvador to Chile to Panama, the United States has treated international law with contempt, propping up vicious despots so that American business could thrive. This contempt went so far as to try to rule the Geneva conventions null and void when it came to Iraq, a move that was overruled by its own court system. Like in the cowboy movies, the law was treated with disdain. The UN was given validity and respect only if it supported the US invasion of Iraq. When it became apparent that the UN Security Council would not pass a resolution supporting military action in Iraq, Bush called the UN "irrelevant", said it was nothing more than a "debating club" and he launched his career as a war criminal. Ever the hypocrite, Bush basked in the role of war hawk, after having turned his cowardly back on Vietnam when it was his turn to serve.

The disrespect for the law that was revealed with the invasion of Iraq is mirrored by the rich and powerful in American society today, and has no better analogy than the financial meltdown of 2008. Despite the fact that millions lost their pension plans, their homes, their jobs and their life savings because of the criminal manipulations of those in charge of America's finances, not one of the perpetrators of that debacle spent a day in court. The only organization actually charged with a crime was a tiny bank in New York that was charged with defrauding Fanny Mae and Freddie Mac. This kind of twisted logic was truly theater of the absurd. Rather than face criminal charges, the bandits of Wall Street were rewarded by George Bush with a federal government bailout of seven hundred billion dollars. This reverse-Robin Hood allocation of financial resources, in which the rich became even richer, was systematic of the Bush philosophy from the time he became president. Although he paid lip service to the military and the brave men and women who died for their country, he thought nothing of cutting funding to military hospitals so that he could reward his friends and relatives, the wealthiest people in America. Two of the more prominent characters in that fiasco on Wall Street, Timothy Geithner and Larry Summers, were actually rewarded with positions in Barack Obama's cabinet, Summers as Director of the National Economic Council and Geithner as Secretary of the Treasury. Both Geithner and Summers were powerful advocates of deregulating the derivatives market, a crucial factor in the financial meltdown. The documentary Inside Job, released in 2010, identified Summers as one of the key figures in the financial meltdown. He was asked by the media at one point if he felt he should apologize to the millions of Americans who lost their jobs, their homes, their savings and their pension plans and he replied arrogantly, "I don't do apologies." Many of the executives who were directly responsible for the financial meltdown received huge bonuses paid from that government bail-out money, and one company that received bail-out money from the federal government used the public funds to take their entire staff to California for rest and relaxation. It was reported that $2.3 billion of the bailout money from taxpayer dollars was paid out as bonuses to the very people who caused the financial crisis in the first place. Geithner played a key role in the bailout of AIG, a company that subsequently paid obscene bonuses to its executives, the very people who caused the melt-down. **36.**

The United States of America has on more than one occasion stated that international law is not applicable to the USA, in particular when it interferes with America's desire to achieve global hegemony. The invasion of Iraq mirrored this attitude of disdain for international law, just as law is disrespected and abused in cowboy movies. The law was a nebulous thing in the Old West and many times cowboys found themselves having to "do what needs to be done". In cowboy movies we see lawmen treated as buffoons, in particular in Butch Cassidy, and we see them treated as being evil, in particular in Open Range and Unforgiven. We also see lawmen being virtually invisible, a favorite movie strategy used by director Quentin Tarantino. In his most famous movie, Pulp Fiction, we saw a plethora of illegal and vicious gang activity but we never saw a policeman. So too in his cowboy movie Django Unchained we see no lawmen performing their duties, despite a cascade of horrible violence throughout the movie. In none of the cowboy movies highlighted here did we see lawmen as respected members of society, upholding the law while acknowledging the principle of universality.

Acts of overt lawlessness were common in the Old West, and none was more infamous than the Johnson County fiasco in 1889 in Wyoming. James Averell and his partner Ella Watson were living on a small homestead that the local cattlemen's association considered "open range". The rich and powerful cattlemen representing the Wyoming Stock Growers Association began their illegal effort to shut those two down by smearing their reputations, spreading the rumor that Averell headed a notorious gang of rustlers and that Watson was a prostitute who sold sexual services for cows. After failing to prove these charges, and failing to drive them off their homestead, a vigilante group of cattlemen simply invaded their ranch and lynched them.

The small ranchers in the area were shocked by the lynching, and decided they had to organize. They formed the Northern Wyoming Farmers and Stockgrowers Association (NWSFA), and in 1892 hired Nathan Champion, a tough trail boss, to lead a drive to take their cattle east. Outraged at these upstarts for challenging the power and control of the Stock Growers Association, fifty gunmen hired by these rich power brokers went into Johnson County. They killed three members of the NWFSA and then trapped Champion in a cabin, where he was eventually smoked out and killed. Although the murderers in both cases were well-known, no charges were laid and they walked free, in the same way that Bush and Cheney walk free today, despite their obvious behavior as war criminals. 37.

George Bush on so many occasions during this invasion of Iraq treated the law with contempt, just as the powerful ranchers in Wyoming had no respect for the law. He tried to go to Congress and change the law retroactively to hide his criminal behavior. He tried to have the Geneva Conventions ruled null and void. He vetoed a law against waterboarding. He started a comprehensive domestic spying program by NSA in which millions of Americans had their emails read, their mail opened, their cell-phone calls logged, all illegal activities without a warrant. Like the cowboys he venerated, Bush saw himself as "doing what needs to be done", and he had no concern for breaking the laws of the American constitution, nor was he concerned with international law. He emulated the cowboy disdain for the law, considered himself to be above the law, and he terrorized the civilian population of Iraq.

CHAPTER 7

....

REVENGE DRIVES THE VIOLENCE

....

"The president has adopted a policy of 'anticipatory self-defence' that is alarmingly similar to the policy that imperial Japan employed at Pearl Harbor.....today it is we Americans who live in infamy."

—ARTHUR SCHLESINGER

After 9/11, Muslims, Arab-Americans and anyone else who looked like a Muslim were targeted by Americans looking for revenge. This national attitude towards vengeance resulted in the fatal shooting of Babir Singh Sodhi, a Sikh who was murdered by Frank Roque. Roque wanted to "kill a Muslim", that being his own revenge response to the terrorist attacks. **1.** Sodhi was not alone in being targeted after 9/11, for Americans struck out at anyone who even resembled a Muslim or an Arab. Attacks on businesses and homes, and personal assaults, became endemic as Americans lashed out with vindictive anger at the misplaced victims of their lust for revenge. Recently, ISIS executed American Kayla Mueller and in revenge, 'patriot' Craig Hicks took his gun and shot in the head and killed 3 young Muslim students attending university in North Carolina. Deah Barakat, Yusor Mohammed and Razan Abu-Salha had no connection to ISIS or al-Qaeda or any other radical Muslim organization, and were just peacefully attending university when their lives were brutally ended by this vengeful gunman's bullets. **2.** In December of 2015 a Muslim couple attacked a luncheon party in San Bernardino, California with machine guns, causing the worst terrorist attack since 9/11. Subsequently, there were attacks of vandalism on Muslim mosques across America. There was even an attack of vandalism on a Sikh temple, the attackers not being aware that there is no connection between Muslims and Sikhs.

In addition to having a national character, revenge was very personal for George W. Bush. At a political fundraiser in Houston, Texas, Bush said, "After all, this is the guy who tried to kill my Dad". He later described an American invasion of Iraq as a deeply American issue, made personal by Saddam's attempt on the life of ex-president George H. W. Bush, his father. President Bill Clinton addressed the U.S. Congress after the April, 1993 attempt on Bush Sr.'s life and declared: "This Thursday, Attorney General Reno and Director of Central Intelligence Woolsey gave me their findings. Based on their investigation there is compelling evidence that there was, in fact, a plot to assassinate former President Bush. This plot, which included the use of a powerful bomb made in Iraq, was directed and pursued by the Iraqi Intelligence Service." 3.

In all of the articles and speeches about Saddam trying to kill George H. W. Bush, there has been no mention of the U.S. military and Bush Sr. deliberately trying to kill Saddam during Gulf War 1. The U.S. military had two 5000 lb. bombs made specifically for Saddam Hussein, the largest non-nuclear bombs ever made. The CIA was tasked with finding where Saddam would be at a certain time and day, and the two bunker-busting bombs were dropped on that location. Fortunately for Saddam, the CIA intelligence was wrong, he wasn't there when the bombs were dropped and the only consequence was the deaths of an untold number of innocent civilians. General John Leide of Coalition Intelligence confirmed that Saddam was a target during Gulf War 1. In total there were 260 bombing raids on Baghdad that were specifically directed at murdering Saddam Hussein. Saddam was simply reacting to the need for revenge himself when he plotted the attack on Bush Sr. while the Bush family was being honored in Kuwait. 4.

Bob Woodward described a cabinet meeting just before the invasion of Iraq when George W. Bush asked around the table, one by one, 'Is this personal?' And everyone said, 'No.' "What a weird moment. Why would it be personal to anyone, except the president himself, who made several public comments about Saddam's attempt on the life of his father? Just before the war in Iraq, Uday Hussein issued a chilling statement. 'Let not he who attacks us think that his mother or children will be safe.' I was watching television when I heard this. And at that moment I knew that not only would Saddam Hussein die, but both of his sons would die as well. George W. Bush knew how danger-ous it would be to leave the sons living. When U. S. forces invaded Baghdad, they occupied the palace of Uday Hussein, and in a room in a basement they found a large collection of pornography. Plastered on the wall was a poster of the Bush twins. The President's two daughters". **5.**

There was both a strong national desire for revenge in America and an intense personal desire on the part of George Bush for revenge. The national desire coalesced around an attack on Iraq because of the sinister manipulations of the Bush regime, which consistently portrayed in public a connection between Iraq and 9/11 that simply did not exist. The concept of revenge is a common theme in cowboy movies, as it is in American culture, and so we see the cowboy president being motivated by revenge as he launched the illegal invasion of Iraq.

In the movie <u>Open Range</u> Boss and Charlie are motivated by revenge when they attack Baxter's men in the woods. They want revenge for the attack on Mose at the general store. Charlie said to Boss, "We owe them for what they did to Mose." After the murder of Mose and the severe injury to Button, Charlie and Boss are motivated even more by revenge and so they go back to Harmonville and provoke a deadly confrontation with Baxter and his men. Charlie says to Sue, "There's payment to be made to them that done this". Earlier, in the café, Boss tells the Marshal that they have a warrant made out for those that killed Mose and injured Button, and tell Marshal Poole, "We aim to enforce it!" Thus the line in the sand is drawn, and the fight for revenge begins.

In <u>Tombstone</u> all of the violence in the movie stems from the need for revenge. The bloody attack on the Mexican police in the opening scene is revenge for the police killing two Cowboys. The crippling of Virgil Earp and the assassination of Morgan Earp are acts of vengeance for the McLaury/Clanton killings that took place at the O.K. Corral. The most famous act of revenge is Wyatt Earp's "revenge ride", when he rides out with his small posse to avenge the attacks on his brothers. In the movie he kills twenty-seven Cowboys during this ride, and in the final act of violence, when Doc kills Ringo, vengeance is also the theme. A member of Wyatt's posse comments after a gun fight with the Cowboys, "If they were my brothers, I'd want revenge too." While Doc is lying in his sick bed, Wyatt asks him what motivates men like Ringo. Doc replied "Revenge." Wyatt asked, "For what?" and Doc said, "For being born." Earp's revenge ride in <u>Tombstone</u> is in many ways similar to George Bush's revenge ride into Iraq, both totally illegal and both having been undertaken to deliver payback to the 'evildoers'.

The plot in the movie <u>Unforgiven</u> begins with an act of revenge, when a cowboy and his friend exact bloody revenge on a prostitute for laughing at the size of his penis. Then the prostitutes offer a bounty on the heads of the cowboys who cut and disfigure the face of their friend. This revenge bounty was what drove the plot of the movie. The violent conclusion to the movie is also driven by revenge, when Will Muny seeks to revenge the torture and murder of his friend Ned. Ned is captured by Little Bill and his posse while on his way home, is tortured brutally and killed, then has his body put on display in front of the local saloon

The cowboy movie <u>Butch Cassidy and the Sundance Kid</u> has a revenge theme that eventually led to Butch and Sundance moving to Bolivia, where they die a violent death. E.H. Harriman is angry with Butch and Sundance for constantly robbing his trains. As an act of revenge, he hires a "dream team" of lawmen and trackers to hunt down and assassinate Butch and Sundance. Harriman makes it personal, insisting that the two bandits be killed rather than having them arrested, much in the same way that George Bush made war with Iraq a personal vendetta.

Django, the main character in the cowboy movie <u>Django Unchained</u>, is motivated by revenge when he helps Schultz murder the Brittle brothers. Django and his wife Broomhilde had been brutalized by the Brittle brothers when they were overseers at a plantation where he was enslaved, ugly scars from the whippings crossing his back. Django and his partner Schultz exact revenge on the Ku Klux Klan members when the Klan attack their wagon. Django also makes the violent and bloody conclusion an act of revenge. When he returns to the Candie mansion to rescue his wife, Broomhilde, he could easily have escaped with no further violence. However, he wants revenge for the violent death of his benefactor, Dr. Schultz, and for the way that his wife was treated as a slave. He wires the Candie mansion with dynamite, kills the rest of Calvin Candie's family and his employees, and then blows up the mansion with the evil Stephen alive but wounded still inside. This final explosion of violence is motivated entirely by revenge.

George Bush is a born-again Christian. He reads the Bible and supposedly believes in its teachings. He wears his religious beliefs openly on his sleeve, and he has asked voters in the past to judge him on the basis of his Christian morality.

Romans 12:19 states, "Never take your own revenge, beloved, but leave room for the wrath of God, for it is written 'Vengeance is mine, I will repay' says the Lord."

In Leviticus 19:18 it is written "Do not seek revenge or bear a grudge against anyone."

Proverbs 20:22 states "Do not say 'I'll pay you back for this wrong.' Wait for the lord and He will avenge you."

These are just three of the many quotes from the Bible that explicitly state that Christians should never be motivated by revenge. George Bush's revenge ride into Iraq was a direct violation of his principles as a Christian, and it identified him both as a hypocrite and a sinner, in the eyes of the Lord. Bush is a 'situational' Christian, adopting the Christian veil only when it is convenient to him.

Revenge is a commonly occurring theme in cowboy movies, and it is commonly a cause for violence in modern American culture. The three most common settings for gun-related mass murder in America occur in schools, in workplaces and in families. In schools such as Columbine and Virginia Tech, the student perpetrators are relative outcasts, and the assassins at Columbine speak in their home-made videos of their hatred for the jocks, or the "cool" kids in school who ignore them or ridicule them. They invariably wanted revenge for the manner in which they were treated. In a recent mass murder at a college in California, the gunman had complained of not being able to find a girl to have sex with, and he murdered several cute co-eds in an act of revenge against all of the girls who rejected him.

In workplaces, those who took guns to their workplace with murder on their minds had previously been fired from their jobs, and they returned seeking revenge for the manner in which they had been mistreated. They often killed their boss, their supervisor, the owner of the company, and any other workers that they deemed responsible for losing their jobs. They were motivated entirely by revenge.

Mass murder within families is virtually always an act of revenge following the break-up of a marriage. The rejected spouse wants revenge, and will seek it not only by killing their partner, but also by killing the children and any other extended family members who are present.

Revenge became a primary theme of the invasion of Iraq from two perspectives. Americans wanted revenge for the 9/11 attack on their country, and George Bush wanted revenge for the assassination attempt on his father's life. Due primarily to the many lies and deceptions used by the Bush regime to convince Americans that Saddam was connected to 9/11, many Americans (over 65%) still believed this lie well after it had been exposed as a fabrication. More remarkable is that in a country that considers itself highly literate and a model democracy, over 60% of college students supported the Bush war policies when it was already well-known that his policies were based on lies and deceptions. 6. This paradox can best be understood when seen through the lens of a lust for revenge, for the atrocity that was 9/11. After watching in horror as the planes slammed into the twin towers, these college students wanted desperately to believe the lies of the Bush regime, so that the murder of Muslims in Iraq could serve as justifiable revenge for 9/11. George Bush's revenge ride into Iraq in fact paralleled Wyatt Earp's revenge ride in Tombstone, both in terms of its illegality and in terms of its bloody and violent consequences. Earp, instead of trying to find and punish the perpetrators of the assaults on his brothers, simply went out and killed any Cowboy he could find. George Bush, instead of punishing the al Qaeda culprits who planned and carried out the 9/11 attacks, simply went to Iraq and killed as many Muslims as he could find. While Americans reveled in the "shock and awe" revenge attacks on Baghdad, imitating as they did the murderous video games popular in America today, the rest of the world was horrified at the carnage instigated by this criminal regime.

Although revenge was a prominent theme of this war, it never should have been, for at no time did George Bush or members of his criminal regime ever have any evidence whatsoever that Iraq had a connection to 9/11, to Osama bin Laden, to al Qaeda or to weapons of mass destruction

CHAPTER 8

MONEY: THE PREDOMINANT GOAL IN AMERICA

"When the rich make war, it's the poor who die."

— JEAN PAUL SARTRE

Jean Paul Sartre was a French philosopher, and as a professional thinker he had many ideas to express about the concept of war. None rings more true than the above statement, for it is never anyone from the Bush family or the Cheney family or the families of their super-rich friends, the people Bush called his base, who serve their country in the military during a time of war. The rich make war so that they can make money, and the profits from Iraq were truly bountiful for the rich in America, with Bush and Cheney serving so well as their frontmen. Michael Moore in his Academy Award winning documentary Fahrenheit 9/11 stood outside Congress and asked congressmen who had voted for the Iraq war if their children had volunteered for the military. The question was rhetorical, for Moore knew beforehand that only one of the children of those 500+ politicians ever joined the military. It was the men and women in Congress who voted for war, but it was not their children who served.

Iraq is well-known to have the second largest oil reserves in the world, after Saudi Arabia, and when the Saudis started making oil deals with China and other countries, the USA turned to Iraq to solve the problem of its own declining reserves of oil. The manipulations of Rumsfeld, Cheney and Wolfowitz between 1996 and 2002 spoke volumes about the attitude of the Bush regime towards invading Iraq. The American oil giants and many American corporations were given no-bid contracts, sweetheart deals given to Shell, Exxon, Halliburton, Blackwater and General Dynamics. These were the kinds of deals you get only if you have friends in high places. Those war profiteers had friends in very high places. It is no coincidence that Bush, Cheney and Rice all had close, long-term connections to Big Oil. In an article that estimated the death toll of Iraqis as a result of the invasion to be

1.2 million, Alan Greenspan, former head of the Federal Reserve under four presidents, was quoted as saying "Everyone knows the Iraq war is largely about oil". **1.**

Going beyond the oil reserves, America's military supply industries and their trillion dollar profits was a monster waiting to be fed, like the proverbial elephant in the room. Money was cascading in front of Bush's eyes as he contemplated the easy road into Iraq. Look hard enough and there is usually a money motive behind illicit activities. Like the previous Republican lawbreaker who served as president, Richard Nixon, who prolonged the Vietnam War for seven long years, Bush was feeding his elite, the very rich in America, by giving them the equally-prolonged war in Iraq. It is a war still in progress, and heading into its 13th year; over $4 trillion has been spent on this war, most of it accruing to defense industry contractors in the USA.

Lockheed-Martin has more than doubled its stock value since the war in Iraq began, while military contractor General Dynamics tripled its profits in that same time frame. General Dynamics had an interesting relationship with Lt. General David Heebner, who in the 1990's was a top aide to Army Chief of Staff Eric Shinseki. The relationship between Heebner and General Dynamics in microcosm serves as an excellent paradigm for the nefarious interconnections between the Bush regime and the military-industrial complex. At the same time that General Dynamics was developing the Stryker, a new light-armored vehicle, and was trying to sell it to the Pentagon, Heebner was negotiating with General Dynamics to leave the military and join its staff. One month after Shinseki approved purchase of this vehicle Heebner left the army to join the staff of General Dynamics, and was rewarded with 33,500 shares in that company, worth over $4 million. **2.** Nice pay-off for a job well-done. Also working for General Dynamics were former Bush-appointed Attorney General John Ashcroft, Cheney's former press secretary Juleanna Weiss, Ashcroft's former assistant Lori Sharp and Willi Gaynor, who worked for the 2004 Bush-Cheney re-election campaign. In a footnote to these shadowy connections, the Stryker was expected to be an essential vehicle during the war in Iraq, but it had serious deficiencies in design, and created a major scandal for the manufacturer because of defaults on the original contract.

The Carlyle Group is a multi-national defense contractor which earned billions from this war in part because of its ownership of General Dynamics. George Bush Sr. shared a position on the Board of Directors of The Carlyle Group with Osama bin Laden's family, heavy investors in The Carlyle Group.

Very thoughtful of George Bush Jr., arranging this war so as to enrich his father, and the bin Laden family, in much the same way that Cheney was able to enrich his friends at Halliburton, and Rice could reward her friends at Big Oil. Will there be an accounting when George Jr. is in a position to inherit his father's wealth, thus directly profiting from the illegal, mercenary war that he himself orchestrated?

In the movie <u>Open Range</u> the money talk begins early, when Boss and Charlie try to get Mose out of jail. Boss asks how much he owes for the fines, and the Marshal says, "How does $50 a charge sound?" Charlie responds by saying, "like robbery", and puts his hand on his gun, delineating the integral connection between violence and money. Baxter, the evil cattle baron, jumps in then and says, "Oh yes, it's a lot of money". Then he introduces himself and immediately starts boasting about how rich he is. "I've got the biggest spread around here, bigger than three or four put together" he said. "Built it up with my own two hands". Baxter then threatens Boss and Charlie and tells them to move on. He isn't going to let any free-graze cattle take the feed off his land. It isn't really his land, but then the oil in Iraq doesn't really belong to Exxon or Shell either. When Charlie, Boss and Mose eventually return to their wagon, Boss says to Charlie, "I know men like Baxter. He means to have this herd". Although Baxter has the largest herd of cattle in the region, Baxter the cattle baron still wants to steal the small herd that Charlie and Boss are driving across the range, and he is willing to shed blood to complete that acquisition, just as George Bush in all his bravery was willing to shed the blood of his brave soldiers so that Exxon and Shell could acquire Iraqi oil. On a smaller scale, Baxter's greed parallels the greed of the richest country in the world as it plundered the oil from a much weaker and much poorer country.

The plot of <u>Butch Cassidy and the Sundance Kid</u> is driven entirely by money, as Butch and Sundance rob and steal throughout the movie. In the opening scene from the movie Butch is standing in front of a bank that had been built like a fortress, making it very difficult to rob. Butch asks the security guard, "What happened to the old bank? It was beautiful!" The guard replies, "People kept robbing it." Obviously disgruntled, Butch mutters, "a small price to pay for beauty." The movie continues with a poker game, a scene we see in so many cowboy movies. Most of the first half of Tombstone had Doc playing poker, or Wyatt dealing faro. When Mose goes missing in <u>Open Range</u>, Boss asks, "Don't suppose he got himself into a poker game?" Money is the predominant theme, just as it is in American culture today, and so we see poker games and bank robberies and train robberies as recurring themes in most cowboy movies.

There is another interesting scene in <u>Butch Cassidy and the Sundance Kid</u> that reinforces this money theme. When Butch uses a bit too much dynamite to blow up the Union Pacific mail car, money is flying into the air, being blown in every direction, and as members of Butch's gang start to gather it up, they notice another train approach. Disembarking from that train is a highly-skilled posse of lawmen, paid to track down and kill Butch and Sundance. Most of the men in the Hole-in-the Wall gang disperse, but two of the greedier outlaws continue to gather the money, as the posse approaches. These two are summarily shot from their saddles and killed, and in the process demonstrate the power of the almighty dollar. Grasping for every last bit of cash floating in the air, even as death is pounding on their doorstep, their lives are consumed by their greed. So many times in cowboy movies we see this value, where money takes precedence over all else, and many times the pursuit of money results in violence and death, just as in American society today.

In the film <u>Unforgiven</u>, Clint Eastwood leaves his two young children to fend for themselves, isolated in a frontier cabin with no means to protect themselves, while he pursues a $500 bounty. Here we see money dominating the plot, and causing the Eastwood character to abandon his young family, to pursue the pot of gold. The prostitutes in the movie raise $1000 as a bounty, thus driving the plot of the movie. English Bob arrives in the town of Big Whiskey, in pursuit of the reward, and is beaten, humiliated and driven away. It is suggested that several other bounty hunters are also interested. The theme of "bounty hunting", or killing men for money, dominates not only this movie but also the more recent <u>Django Unchained</u>. The "dream team" posse put together by E.L.

Harriman in <u>Butch Cassidy and the Sundance Kid</u> are also bounty hunters, sent out to kill for money. In <u>Unforgiven</u> the bounty on the two cowboys eventually causes the death of Ned (Morgan Freeman), Clint's only friend, it causes the deaths of the two cowboys and Little Bill, and it causes the violent and deadly shoot-out that ends the movie.

In <u>Tombstone</u>, the entire plot is driven by Wyatt's desire to make money. He meets his brothers and they move to Tombstone for the express purpose of exploiting the new-found riches from the silver mines. Wyatt turns down the marshaling job in the first town he is in, and is challenged with the accusation "Going to Tombstone to strike it rich?" When asked if that would give him a guilty conscience, he replies, "I already have a guilty conscience. I might as well have the money too." When he and his brothers Virgil and Morgan first arrive in Tombstone, their initial comments are all about how rich the town seems to be, and how they are going to "loot this burg!" Wyatt's brother Morgan says, "You can smell the silver in this town." Wyatt sets himself up as a faro dealer, gets himself a quarter interest in the saloon, and then lets Curley Bill Brocious win $500 in one turn of the cards, in order to defuse a potentially violent confrontation. It seems that every scene revolves around money. One of our heroes, Doc Holliday, is a professional gambler and is seen in one of the opening scenes stealing money from a saloon, before he leaves town. This scene parallels the opening scene in <u>Butch Cassidy and the Sundance Kid</u>, when Sundance is playing poker and is accused of cheating, just as Doc is accused of cheating at the beginning of Tombstone. The entire plot of <u>Tombstone</u> revolves around money, and when Johnny Ringo challenges Wyatt to a gunfight, Wyatt retorts, "I'm not going to fight you Ringo. There's no money in it". This confrontation underlines one of the integral themes in the movie. Every time the Earp brothers discuss their next move, money comes into play. Wyatt says to Mattie, "We've already made a pile of money in this place" when contemplating leaving Tombstone. When the Mayor approaches Wyatt about becoming Marshal in Tombstone, he says "You men are making a lot of money in this town." At the conclusion of the movie Wyatt proposes to Josie, and then confesses he has no money. Josie replies, "Don't worry about it, Wyatt. My family is rich!" Every part of the plot is driven by money, by the love of money and by the need to have more.

One of the most famous westerns from the 1960's is Sergio Leone's third spaghetti western, <u>The Good, the Bad and the Ugly</u>, starring Clint Eastwood,

Lee Van Cleef and Eli Wallach. More than one fan of western movies has ranked this film the best western ever. It was most certainly Eastwood's ticket to Hollywood. In this movie, as in the other two movies in this trilogy, the plot is driven entirely by money. "Blondie" and Tuco are running a scam where Blondie repeatedly turns Tuco in for the reward and then frees him by shooting the hangman's noose. They learn of a box of gold coins worth $200,000 buried in a graveyard, and this becomes the obsession not only of Blondie and Tuco but also of the evil "Angel Eyes", played by Lee Van Cleef. Leone's spaghetti western trilogy has been labelled "nihilistic", because the characters aren't bound by any moral or ethical code. They're just driven by greed, but that is no different than many of the characters in western movies; they want to get as much money or gold as they can with little concern for the means to that end. Thus cowboy movies center around bank robberies, poker games, stagecoach robberies, cattle rustling and the many conflicts between the rich, powerful ranchers and the less wealthy townspeople, merchants and itinerant cowboys.

The first two movies in Sergio Leone's trilogy are called <u>A Fistful of Dollars</u> and <u>For a Few Dollars More</u>, the titles leaving little doubt as to the controlling theme. They reflect the controlling theme in most cowboy movies, including the latest cowboy movie nominated for Best Picture in 2012, <u>Django Unchained</u>. In this latest cowboy mega-hit, Dr. Shultz and Django act as bounty hunters in the early part of the film, and kill men for money. Money is also the key to the second half of the movie, as Shultz negotiates to buy from Calvin Candie a fighting Mandingo slave for $12,000, a subterfuge aimed at freeing Django's wife. Shultz ends up paying the Mandingo price for Django's wife when their scam is revealed, by giving the entire $12,000 for her freedom, when in fact a female slave is worth only a fraction of that amount. Towards the end of the movie Django is held prisoner and is being taken to spend the rest of his days in a mine. He is able to manipulate the greed of his captors by offering them a chance to collect a lucrative bounty, and cons them into releasing him. Of course there is no bounty and Django kills his captors, before freeing his wife. Money and greed drive the entire plot of this movie also.

Brown University sponsored a <u>Cost of War Project</u> conducted by the <u>Watson Institute for International Studies</u>. Their latest estimate as of April 15, 2016 is that the war in Iraq has cost the American people over $4.4 trillion at this point. This does not include $490 billion in immediate benefits owed to military veterans, and untold billions in lifetime benefits owed to veterans.

We know where this $4.4 trillion dollars came from-the American people and the tax dollars they send to Washington. Where did this $4.4 trillion in expenditures go? Well, over $60 billion went the way of graft and corruption, according to the Commission on Wartime Contracting. American taxpayers paid $60 billion for- nothing. Alan Grayson was the Florida-based attorney prosecuting "Coalition Provisional Authority" corruption. He said:

"American law was suspended, Iraqi law was suspended, and Iraq basically became a free fraud zone. In a free fire zone you can shoot at anybody you want. In a free fraud zone you can steal anything you like. And that's what they did." At one point $12 billion in cash was shrink-wrapped and shipped to Baghdad. $9 billion of that $12 billion simply disappeared, with no one held to account for its disappearance.

The Halliburton Corporation has taken a large chunk of the money spent in Iraq, over $50 billion so far, this at a time when Dick Cheney, ex-CEO of Halliburton, was earning $200,000 a year from Halliburton, and still holding over $10 million in stock options for Halliburton. He received this salary and held these shares and arrogantly refused to divest himself of them during this obvious conflict of interest, while he made major decisions about a war that enriched both himself and his friends at Halliburton. His hubris underlined the complete lack of integrity or morality, and the insipid arrogance that Cheney displayed throughout the debacle that was the war in Iraq. Many of the contracts awarded to Halliburton were given without competitive bidding, like gifts from a friendly Vice President. One recent contract given to Halliburton for $568 million for housing, meals and bathroom facilities for soldiers was one of many awarded without bids from competing firms, and it led to a subsequent lawsuit filed by the justice department for kickbacks. Cheney's lack of character is reflected both in the blatant lies he told in the months preceding the invasion, and in the small fortune he earned from the war that he created.

Just as money dominated cowboy movies, it also dominated the rationale for invading Iraq. Violence to solve problems, good guy/bad guy rhetoric, revenge and contempt for the law were the cowboy values that drove the process of invading Iraq to the ultimate devastation of that country. However, money was the dominating theme, in particular the money accrued through the military-industrial complex. Dick Cheney had his close ties to Halliburton, John Ashcroft had his close link to General Dynamics, Condoleezza Rice had business connections to Big Oil, sitting on the Board of Directors of Chevron Corporation, and even having an oil tanker named after her for all her hard work on their behalf. George Bush was closely connected to the war profiteers through his father's position with The Carlyle Group, and through all of his earlier connections to the oil industry. Each of the major military contractors, including Halliburton, Blackwater, The Carlyle Group, General Dynamics, Lockheed-Martin, and the Big Oil beneficiaries Exxon and Shell, made obscene profits from the war in Iraq. It is these profits that more than any other single factor explains the real rationale for the invasion of Iraq. Said Bush to a group of multi-millionaires, many of whom owned millions of dollars in shares in corporations that profited enormously from the war, "This is an impressive crowd-the haves and have-mores. Some people call you the elite. I call you my base." 4.

It was no secret that Bush considered the very rich in America to be the source of his support. He consistently made tax cuts for the most wealthy as the primary motive in his budgets, with one tax cut providing $350 billion in tax relief for the very rich, at the same time that cutbacks in spending were made to military hospitals for wounded veterans. His family, his friends, his neighbors, his colleagues in government, and the many corporate power-brokers who contributed to his campaigns for president all profited immensely from the war in Iraq, just as they profited previously from Nixon's ability to stretch out the Vietnam war for so many years. The rich knew where their profits came from, and as they looked to George Bush to enrich their already-bloated portfolios, he created this war just for them.

One soldier was very blunt in his assessment of the role that money plays in the military actions that America undertakes. Major-General Smedley Butler in his memoirs stated, "War is a racket. The few profit, the many pay. I was a racketeer for capitalism" In addition to being a racketeer for capitalism, Smedley Butler was a senior commander in the US military during the time of World War 1, and was part of an invasion force that entered Haiti in 1915. He was tasked by President Woodrow Wilson with disbanding the Haitian parliament at gunpoint, because the democratically-elected lawmakers in Haiti refused to adopt a U.S.-imposed constitution permitting American corporations to purchase land in Haiti. Butler then supervised a referendum in which 99% of the voters approved the U.S.-imposed constitution. Less than 5% of the population actually voted, those being the wealthier citizens of Haiti, most of whom had financial connections to the American corporations. That statistic was ignored by the media in America as they lauded this American-imposed exercise in democracy. When it came to the imposition of democratic values, as a forerunner to the acquisition of wealth, the hypocrisy of the power elite in America knew no bounds.

Butler said: "I helped make Mexico and especially Tampico safe for American oil interests in 1914. I helped make Haiti and Cuba a decent place for the National City Bank boys to collect revenues in. I helped in the raping of half a dozen Central American republics for the benefit of Wall Street. The record of racketeering is long. I helped purify Nicaragua for the international banking house of Brown Brothers 1909-12. I brought light to the Dominican Republic for American sugar interests in 1910. I helped make Honduras "right" for American fruit companies in 1903. In China in 1927 I helped see to it that Standard Oil went its way unmolested." 5. Nothing changed with the invasion of Iraq, as defense industry contractors earned enormous profits, dealing away the dead and mutilated bodies of America's soldiers for some cold, hard cash. Few of those soldiers realized that the invasion of Iraq was an exercise in American capitalism. Any doubt that money played a key role in the invasion of Iraq was resolved when Dow Jones announced in 2007 that a law drawn up by the Bush government and presented for debate to the Iraqi "puppet" parliament would give Western oil companies (Shell, Exxon) thirty year contracts to extract Iraqi oil. The contracts stated that 75% of the profits would go to the foreign companies, a drastic increase from the 10% figure in other oil-producing countries in the Middle East. **6.**

Dr. Norman Bethune, a Canadian heart surgeon and inventor, was in China during Japan's bloody and destructive war of aggression there in the 1930's. Bethune's comments about that war apply with even more validity to America's recent assault on Iraq. Transpose in Bethune's remarks Iraq and America for China and Japan, and his words ring as true now as they did in the 1930's.

"What is the cause of this cruelty, this stupidity? A few hundred thousand soldiers come from America to kill half a million Iraqi citizens. Why should the American soldier attack the Iraqi, who is forced merely to defend himself? Will the American soldier benefit by the death of the Iraqi? No, how can he gain? Then, in God's name, who will gain? Who is responsible for sending these American soldiers on this murderous mission? Who will profit from it? Is it possible that a few rich men, a small class of men, have persuaded several hundred thousand men to attack, and attempt to destroy, another half a million men as poor as they? So that these rich may be richer still? How did they persuade these poor men to go to Iraq? By telling them the truth? No, they would never have gone if they had known the truth. Did they dare to tell these soldiers that the rich only wanted cheaper raw materials and more profit? The agents of an easy criminal war of aggression, such as this, must be looked for like the agents of other crimes, such as murder, among those who are likely to benefit from those crimes. Will the workers of America, the poor, the unemployed industrial workers — will they gain? No!! So how are they likely to benefit by the armed robbery of the oil from Iraq? Will not the rich owners of the one retain for their own profit the wealth of the other? Have they not always done so? It would seem inescapable that the militarists and the capitalists of America are the only class likely to gain by this mass murder, this authorized madness, this sanctified butchery. They make war to capture markets by murder; raw materials by rape. They find it cheaper to steal than to exchange; easier to butcher than to buy. This is the secret of war. This is the secret of all wars."

The American soldiers thought they were fighting to protect their country from weapons of mass destruction in the Middle East, and to get revenge for 9/11. Did George Bush tell these soldiers the truth before sending them to die? Would American soldiers have gone to Iraq if they'd known that the purpose of the war was to enrich General Dynamics and Halliburton and The Carlyle Group, and in the process make a fortune for Dick Cheney and his friends? Would they have gone to Iraq at the behest of Condoleezza Rice's good friends at Exxon and Shell, companies that were thirsting for Iraqi oil? Would they have gone had they known that the military-industrial complex, about which Eisenhower warned us 65 years ago, was to be the primary recipient of the $4.4 trillion in tax dollars given over to the blood-lust that was the Iraq war?

Dwight D. Eisenhower, as a soldier and then as the thirty-fourth President of the United States, knew the savage and inhumane consequences of war, and he knew who profited from it. When he stepped down from the presidency, he warned America about the military-industrial complex and how it was controlling the agenda in the White House. He said:

"Every gun that is made, every warship launched, every rocket fired signifies, in the final sense, a theft from those who hunger and are not fed, those who are cold and are not clothed. This world in arms is not spending money alone. It is spending the sweat of its laborers, the genius of its scientists, and the hopes of its children. This is not a way of life at all in the true sense. Under the clouds of war, it is humanity hanging on an iron cross." 7.

In his final speech to the America people in 1961, Eisenhower said:

"America's leadership and prestige depend not merely on our material progress, and military strength, but also on how we use our power <u>in the interests of world peace and human betterment.</u> Throughout America's adventure in free government, our basic purposes have been to <u>keep the peace</u>, to foster progress in human achievement and to enhance liberty, dignity and integrity among people and among nations." 8.

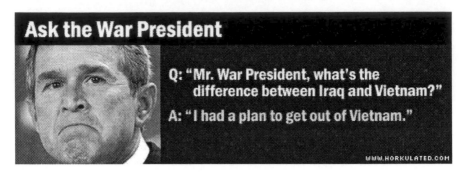

Ask the War President

Q: "Mr. War President, what's the difference between Iraq and Vietnam?"

A: "I had a plan to get out of Vietnam."

WWW.HORKULATED.COM

How sad that George Bush could stray so far from these ideals set out by his fellow Republican, 5-star general and president Dwight D. Eisenhower. One need only examine and compare the extensive and honorable war record of Eisenhower, to the pusillanimous war record of draft dodger George Bush during the Vietnam War, to understand this dichotomy.

The immense video-game missiles fired into Bagdad in March of 2003 were worth approximately one million dollars apiece, and they weren't making anyone any money unless they were used. When trillions of dollars were at stake, and "shock and awe" was blazing from the scoreboard, the lives of over 4500 brave young men and women in the American military were nothing to expend, a triviality. The shattered lives of those many tens of thousands of debilitated American soldiers languishing in under-funded military hospitals were but a small but necessary expenditure in order to reap the fantastic profits of war. Badly injured veterans were languishing in hallways, without a bed, while America's rich wallowed in the lap of luxury, bestowed on them by the magnanimous generosity of the Bush tax cuts and the Bush war expenditures.

Alexis de Tocqueville stated in his book "On Democracy in America";

"As one digs deeper into the national character of the Americans, one sees that they have sought the value of everything in this world only in the answer to this single question: how much money will it bring in?"

Calculating the many billions of dollars that Halliburton, Blackwater, Exxon, Shell, General Dynamics and The Carlyle Group have earned so far from Iraq, and then considering the profits made by so many other members of that very exclusive club, the military-industrial complex, one can see that the balance sheet is very much tilted in favor of America's rich and powerful. These were

George Bush's people, the very rich in America, his base, and he created this war just for them.

Pope Francis, the inspirational leader of the Catholic Church, addressed the current violent conflict in Syria and Iraq on November 20, 2015. He could well have been talking directly to George Bush and Dick Cheney, when he asked:

"What shall remain in the wake of this war, in the midst of which we are now living? What shall remain? Ruins, thousands of children without education, so many innocent victims, and lots of money in the pockets of arms dealers. We should weep for those (Bush-Cheney) who love for war, and have the cynicism to deny it." **9.**

The impetus to invade Iraq began with the American belief that violence is an accepted and viable solution to conflict. It was solidified with the Bush emphasis on a good vs evil paradigm, validation came with the complete disregard for international law, including a blatant disregard for the American constitution, disrespect for the Geneva conventions, contempt for the constitution of the United Nations and indifference to the Nuremburg protocols established after World War Two. The revenge card was played to great effect, both on a personal level by Mr. Bush and on a national level when Bush and Cheney lied to the American people, and to Congress, about the connection between Iraq and 9/11. Cementing the forward march to war was the money to be made by friends of the Bush administration, both from the oil they intended to expropriate and from the obscene profits accruing to the military-industrial complex. What has followed from the devastation of Iraq is total uproar and vast uncertainty in the Middle East, with 65 nations waging war in Iraq and Syria, civil war in Yemen involving Saudi Arabia and Iran, continued animosity and violence between Palestinians and Israelis, terrible violence in Africa spawned by al Qaeda and ISIS associates, and a continuing war in Afghanistan that has created terrible devastation to the civilian population. Overshadowing all of that turmoil is the ever-increasing threat of nuclear war, a looming catastrophe that has been created and produced by George W. Bush, Dick Cheney and their blood-thirsty regime in the White House.

CHAPTER 9

· ·

THE FALLOUT FROM IRAQ: WILL IT BE NUCLEAR?

· ·

"The unleashed power of the atom has changed everything, except the way that we think, and so we drift towards unparalleled catastrophe."

— ALBERT EINSTEIN

On July 10, 1955 two of the great minds of the 20th century issued a dire warning to the world. In a letter to the New York Times, Bertrand Russell and Albert Einstein stated that the world is facing a choice that is "stark and dreadful and inescapable: shall we put an end to the human race; or shall mankind renounce war?"

The United States of America wasn't listening, and so we wonder if the fallout from Iraq could possibly be nuclear. The threat of a nuclear holocaust is far more likely to emanate from American foreign policy than from anything Saddam Hussein, Osama bin Laden or any of their successors ever did. Congress and the Presidency have supported treasury-draining, scientific research into anti-missile systems, nuclear bunker-busting weapons and a whole new arsenal of mini-nuclear weapons, including the most expensive program in the world in support of weapons in space. There is a treaty in place among most nations who have nuclear weapons. That treaty calls on the signees not to ever be the nation to use nuclear weapons first. This "first-use" clause is part of a world-wide effort to prevent nuclear holocaust. The United States and American client-state Israel are the only nuclear countries not to sign that treaty. Israel continues to deny having nuclear weapons, despite having at its disposal the third largest nuclear arsenal in the world.

In 2002 defense analyst William Arkin reported that the Bush administration had developed a new program called "Global Strike". Contingency Plan 8022 described preventative and pre-emptive attacks including a nuclear attack option. **1.** On January 10, 2003 Bush defined Global Strike as "a capability to deliver rapid extended range precision nuclear weapons in support of national objectives". **2.** In March of 2005 the Joint Chiefs of Staff published a document called Doctrine for Joint Nuclear Operations which established a rationale for use of nuclear weapons. This rationale included the following situations in which nuclear weapons could be used by the United States military;

1. Against an adversary intending to use Weapons of Mass Destruction against the United States, multinational or allied forces or civilian populations.

2. In the event of an imminent attack by biological weapons that only nuclear weapons can destroy.

3. To attack deep, hardened bunkers containing chemical or biological weapons, or the command and control infrastructure required for the adversary to execute a WMD attack against the United States or its friends or allies.

4. To overcome a potentially overwhelming adversary's conventional weapons.

5. For rapid and favorable war termination on U.S. terms.

6. To ensure the success of U.S. and multinational operations. **3.**

This document acknowledges that the U.S military under George Bush was prepared to use nuclear weapons first, against a non-nuclear country, before any hostilities had actually begun. Given this administration's ability to brazenly lie about potential threats from supposed enemies, this shopping list sanctions the use of nuclear weapons virtually anytime and anywhere

In 2001, Bush announced that the United States would withdraw from the Anti-Ballistic Missile Treaty (ABM) and would no longer take part in strategic arms control talks. Bush stated that the ABM treaty "does not recognize the present or point us to the future. It enshrines the past". **4.** In order to facilitate this new reality, Bush hired Keith Payne to be in charge of the "Nuclear Policy Review". As head of the National Institute for Public Policy, Payne had previously written a foreign policy piece titled Victory is Possible, which outlined how a nuclear war with Russia was "winnable", estimating that U.S. civilian casualties would amount to no more than 20-30 million, an acceptable loss according to Payne. Payne was later appointed by George W. Bush as Deputy-Assistant Minister of Defense for Nuclear Forces Policy, giving him total responsibility for nuclear force planning. Bush's new strategic framework was designed to fight nothing less than an all-out nuclear war with Russia or China, abandoning the concept of "mutual assured destruction". 5. Instead of diminishing the role of weapons that no president had ever wanted to use, Bush was advocating the convenient use of nuclear weapons against much lesser threats. The nuclear arsenal in the U.S.A is the most fearsome collection of weapons of mass destruction in the world, making claims about Iraq's supposed WMD the ultimate in hypocrisy.

Close to 50% of all the scientists in the world today, many of them American, work in the military-industrial industries, trying with all of their scientific skills and abilities to perfect ways in which human beings can slaughter one another. Who needs a cure for cancer, when we can have a fancy, new computer-driven drone that can wipe out an entire Pakistani wedding party by remote control, from thousands of miles away, in a matter of minutes? Americans are so good at antiseptic, hands-off forms of murder.

The United States spends almost as much on its military as all of the other countries in the world combined. When China advertises that it has built a new submarine, or a new aircraft carrier, the American media becomes apoplectic at this dire threat to world peace, as if America didn't have 10 or 12 or 15 of whatever it was China just manufactured for the first time. As if China has been 1/100th as threatening to world peace as America has been during the past 50 years. A few years ago, China blew up an old satellite that was floating around uselessly in space. The press in the USA, the White House and the Pentagon all reacted hysterically, saying that China was militarizing space. As of 2004, the USA accounted for 95% of total global military space expenditures worldwide. China's share was something in the vicinity of 1%.

Every mention of a Chinese or a Russian military advancement, however microscopic, is like music to the collective ears of the military-industrial complex in America, for there is nothing more effective in stopping cutbacks to the bloated military budget in the USA than these phantom threats from other countries. The Pentagon maintains an empire of military bases so large and shadowy that no one, not even the Pentagon itself, knows the exact size and scope of US military bases abroad. Rumors hint at a number much larger than 1000. American soldiers are stationed in 144 countries around the world. The United States glories in its hegemony as it sits astride the globe, ever-ready to mete out its own perverted idea of justice to any defenceless nation that doesn't follow the American agenda.

America thrives on enemies just as it thrives on war, for without fearsome enemies to protect against, how could trillion dollar expenditures be justified? Halliburton, General Electric and The Carlyle Group would wither up and die if their friends and relatives in the White House weren't creating situations in which blood could be exchanged for money. This is the dark side of George W. Bush and the war criminals that were part of his regime. This fundamentalist Christian hypocrite, who waged his cowboy war in the Middle East with child-like insouciance, always with that idiot smirk on his face, was leading the world ever-closer to that grim scenario referred to by Einstein and Russell, without a clue as to his actual role in that larger nightmare.

Michael MacGuire, a prominent strategic analyst, has warned of nuclear catastrophe in the wake of the Iraqi invasion. He said;

"There were many reasons-political, military, legal, ethical and economic- for concluding that the decision to wage war on Iraq was fundamentally flawed. But in the longer term, by far the most important was that such an operation threatened to undermine the very fabric of international relations. That decision repudiated a century of slow, intermittent and often painful progress towards an international system based on cooperative security, multilateral decision-making, collective action, agreed norms of behavior and a steadily growing fabric of law." **6.**

In a major speech to his nation, George Bush said, "Free nations are peaceful nations. Free nations don't attack each other. Free nations don't develop weapons of mass destruction." **8.** In fact the United States is guilty of all three, more guilty than any other country in the world. The United States has been in a continual state of war for almost 100 years. A list of the countries it has attacked or invaded since 1900 would fill an entire chapter in this book. Just in the last 20 years, the United States has conducted military action against Afghanistan, Bosnia, Columbia, Haiti, Iraq, Liberia, Libya, Macedonia, Pakistan, the Philippines, Somalia, Sudan, Syria, Yemen, Yugoslavia and Zaire. How does the Bush lecture about "free nations" rationalize these military excursions? Bush asserts that "free nations" don't develop weapons of mass destruction, yet the United States has more weapons of mass destruction than all of the other countries in the world combined. The United States is the only country in the world to have used nuclear weapons in war, it has aided and abetted both India and Israel in their acquisition of nuclear weapons, and it is continuing to develop smaller "strategic" nuclear weapons as it thumbs its arrogant nose at the Nuclear Proliferation Treaty. The United States leads the world in programs designed for the militarization of space, yet another area of WMD enhancement that exceeds in money spent all of the other countries in the world combined. The United States has some of the largest stockpiles of chemical and biological weapons in the world, and provided Saddam with the chemical weapons he used to attack both Iran and his own people, the Kurds. Free nations don't develop weapons of mass destruction? The United States holds the patent on that nefarious activity. George Bush would have done well to heed the words of Eisenhower, who said: "In the councils of government, we must guard against the acquisition of unwarranted influence, whether sought or unsought, by the military-industrial complex. The potential for the disastrous rise of misplaced power exists and will persist." **9.**

Earlier in this chapter, it was suggested that the Bush invasion of Iraq increased the possibility of a nuclear holocaust. Why is nuclear holocaust a possible long-term consequence of this brutal war? We begin with the observation that the United States has the most powerful military arsenal in the world, including a nuclear arsenal that is larger than all other nuclear countries combined. America has shown more willingness, and preparedness, to use nuclear weapons than any other country in the world. Add to these two factors the reality that over the past 100 years America has fought more wars, against more different nations, than any other country in the world. Following these observations, we only have to ask ourselves, would the United States have actually launched its illegal and immoral assault on Iraq if that country actually had a significant nuclear arsenal? The Americans started this war not because Iraq had weapons of mass destruction, in the form of a nuclear arsenal, but precisely because Iraq didn't have any weapons of mass destruction. Now we need to ask ourselves what effect the invasion has had on the nuclear inclinations of Iran, Syria, North Korea, Libya, Indonesia, Egypt, South Africa or any of a host of smaller countries in the world that want the protection that nuclear weapons would offer them. The citizens of Indonesia, with the largest Muslim population in the world, have responded in a poll that they already fear an invasion by America more than any other threat to their country. Should they not arm themselves with nuclear weapons, as a deterrent? Pakistan has already developed a nuclear arsenal, as has India. Why shouldn't these two countries bolster their nuclear arsenals also, in order to create an even stronger deterrent against attack? Pakistan has in fact done just that, after watching how Iraq has been laid to waste.

All of these countries have witnessed America's naked aggression against Iraq, and they have seen the follow-up devastation in that country. Who is to say that the events in Iraq won't inspire a whole new wave of nuclear proliferation, especially given America's contempt for the Nuclear Proliferation Treaty? The United States has repeatedly condemned Iraq, North Korea and Iran for attempting to develop a nuclear arsenal, calling them "the Axis of Evil", yet it openly assisted India in its acquisition of a nuclear arsenal, and it has continuously supported its client state Israel while that country developed the 3rd largest nuclear arsenal in the world. America's general contempt for international law, and its willingness to use raw aggression and brutal violence, together with its abrogation of responsibility for the Nuclear Proliferation Treaty, the First-Use treaty and the Anti-Ballistic Missile treaty, should inspire fear in any country, big or small.

Jimmy Carter, ex-president and winner of the Nobel Peace Prize, stated about the Bush government's approach to the proliferation of nuclear weapons:

"The United States is the major culprit in this erosion of the Nuclear Proliferation Treaty. While claiming to be protecting the world from proliferation threats in Iraq, Libya, Iran and North Korea, American leaders have not only abandoned existing treaty restraints but also have asserted plans to test and develop new weapons, including anti-ballistic missiles, earth-penetrating "bunker-busters" and new smaller (nuclear) bombs. They have also abandoned past pledges and now threaten first use of nuclear weapons against non-nuclear states." 10.

Thomas Graham, who worked as Bill Clinton's special representative for arms control, warned that "the Nuclear Proliferation Treaty has never seemed weaker, or the future less certain." Graham and a number of other analysts have recognized that the primary threat to the NPT is U.S. government policy. He suggested that if the treaty should fail, "a nuclear nightmare world may well become reality".11.

The invasion of Iraq, while superficially designed to control and defuse nuclear weapons, in fact created an environment in which the proliferation of nuclear weapons around the world could exceed anything since the first Nuclear

Proliferation Treaty was signed. Condoleezza Rice may have been correct when she expressed fear of a "mushroom cloud", but it is far more likely to be a cloud created by American policy, than by anything that Islamic terrorists might create.

Albert Einstein best encapsulated the terrorist, nuclear world of George W. Bush when he said:

"I know not with what weapons World War III will be fought, but World War IV will be fought with sticks and stones."

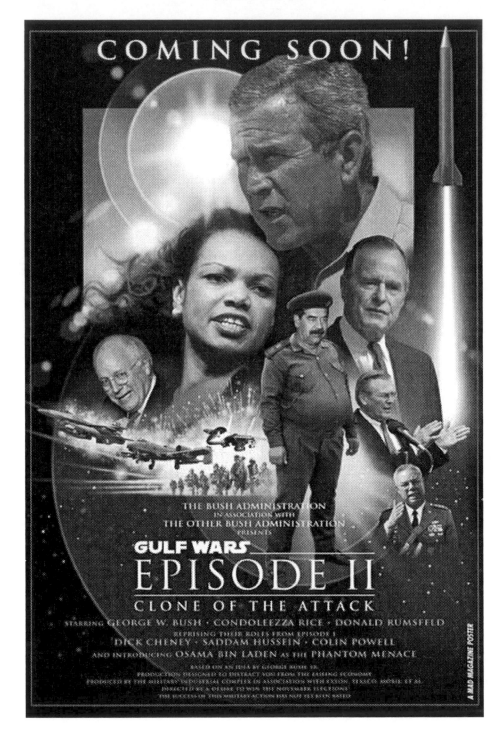

CHAPTER 10

IS GEORGE BUSH A REAL COWBOY?

"It still confuses many Americans that, in a world full of vicious slime-balls, we're about to bomb one that didn't attack us on 9/11 (like Osama), that isn't intercepting our planes (like North Korea), that isn't financing al Qaeda (like Saudi Arabia), that isn't home to Osama (like Pakistan), that isn't a host for terrorists (like Iran, Lebanon and Syria)."

—MAUREEN DOWD IN <u>BUSH: THE XANAX COWBOY</u>

Given that his cowboy persona played a significant role in his attack on Iraq, the question arises as to whether George W. Bush actually is a real cowboy, in the traditional sense of the word. He has embraced that role publicly and with great enthusiasm, but has he in fact honestly portrayed the values inherent in the image of the iconic American cowboy?

Gene Autry was one of the great Hollywood cowboys, and his "cowboy code" is considered to be the most succinct and accurate summation of the values inherent in the traditional cowboy image. Has George Bush measured up to those standards set by the great Gene Autry?

From 1934 to 1953, Autry appeared in 93 cowboy films and 91 episodes of his cowboy television series. During the 1930s and 1940s, he personified the straight-shooting hero—honest, brave, and true—and profoundly touched the lives of millions of Americans. Autry was also one of the most important figures in the history of country and western music, considered the second most influential artist affecting the genre's development after Jimmy Rodgers. His singing cowboy movies were the first vehicle to carry country music to a national audience. He was inducted into the Country Music Hall of Fame in 1969 and the Nashville Songwriters Hall of Fame in 1970. Unlike Bush, who avoided serving his country in Vietnam, Autry served with distinction as a pilot in World War Two, flying cargo planes over the dangerous Himalayas to America's allies in China. **1.**

Autry established his cowboy code in 1949, and those ten principles were the guidelines for all of his movies. The principles were:

1. The Cowboy must never shoot first, hit a smaller man, or take unfair advantage.

2. He must never go back on his word, or a trust confided in him.

3. He must always tell the truth.

4. He must be gentle with children, the elderly, and animals.

5. He must not advocate or possess racially or religiously intolerant ideas.

6. He must help people in distress.

7. He must be a good worker.

8. He must keep himself clean in thought, speech, action, and personal habits.

9. He must respect women, parents, and his nation's laws.

10. The Cowboy is a patriot. **2.**

Bush violated at least 6 of these essential tenets of the cowboy code in a most outrageous fashion with his invasion of Iraq. He attacked a nation that was far smaller and much, much weaker than America. Iraq is 1/10th the size of the USA in land area, barely the size of California, and has 1/10th the population. The per capita GDP in America is $49,922, while the per capita GDP in Iraq is less than $7000. The United States spends almost as much on its technologically advanced military as all of the other countries in the world combined, while Iraq's military was decimated in the first Gulf War, a fact noted by the Pentagon, and was further pulverized by bombing raids in 1998, and the 22,000 bombing raids flown by British and American pilots in 2002. The United States with its invasion of Iraq attacked a much smaller country, shot first and shot often, and took unfair advantage of a very weak nation, all obvious contradictions of Gene Autry's code. Real cowboys are not bullies.

Bush violated the trust placed in him by the soldiers in America's military by putting them in harm's way just to enrich his people, the power elite in America. Soldiers should be able to trust their leaders that if they are put in harm's way, it is for an honest and necessary reason. They could not trust

George Bush or Dick Cheney. This was a violation of principle #2. Bush also violated the trust of the American people by dragging them into a war that was totally unnecessary and totally illegal, by driving up the national debt and by causing international repugnance towards his country.

George Bush lied repeatedly to the American public about his reasons for going to war, a violation of principle #3. He lied about the torture being done with his approval. He lied about the connection between Saddam Hussein and 9/11 and he lied about Iraq's weapons of mass destruction. Earlier, when he was running for president he lied about his military record. Bush lied about wanting to sign up for Vietnam but being rejected, and he lied about his record as a pilot for the National Guard.

With his invasion of Iraq, Bush killed tens of thousands of Iraqi children, the elderly and so many others, in particular with the deliberate mass slaughter of the elderly, women and children in Fallujah, a malevolent violation of principle #4. The Bush regime detained in its various prisons and tortured 2400 children, according to the United Nations Committee on the Rights of Children. Twenty-one children were detained at Guantanamo, where they were jailed with adults, given no access to legal counsel and were routinely tortured. With Bush approval, Khalid Sheik Mohammed's two children, aged 7 and 9, were imprisoned and threatened with torture in order to coerce a confession from him. Fifteen year old Canadian Omar Kadr was put into solitary confinement and tortured repeatedly at Guantanamo. Rapes were reported of both male and female children incarcerated in American prisons. The Guantanamo torturers were following orders from the White House based on George Bush's executive order of February 7, 2002. Bush violated Autry's 4th principal in a most brutal way, violating not just Autry's code but the essential principles of his Christian religion with his brutality against children and the elderly.

When it comes to principle #5, the principle of advocating or possessing religiously intolerant ideas, Bush contradicted it both by his words and by his actions as commander-in-chief. Referring to the conflict in the Middle East as a "crusade" awakened in many people's minds the history of bloody conflict between Muslims and Christians during the Crusades of 800 years ago. Bush's repeated reference to 'Islamic terrorists' and 'Islamofascism' only inflamed religious hatred. Bush repeatedly compared terrorists to Godless communists, again taking a swipe at the Islamic faith. To many Americans the good vs evil framework assumed that Christian America was good and blessed by God, in stark contrast to the evil of Islam.

In 2004 the al-Hassan Mosque was destroyed in a US military bombing raid, and shortly after that forty Muslim worshippers were killed when a 500-lb bomb demolished the Abchel-Aziz al-Samarrai Mosque in Iraq. Over sixty Islamic mosques have been destroyed in Iraq since the war began. Given the claims of both Rumsfeld and Bush in regard to the precision and accuracy of US military bombing raids, one can only assume that Islam itself was being targeted through the destruction of its churches. Advocating and possessing religiously intolerant ideas also included the torture regimes at Kanduhar and al-Ghraib prisons, approved by Bush, in which copies of the sacred text the Qu'an were dropped into toilet buckets, had obscene words scrawled on the pages, were carried around in the mouths of dogs and in other ways were desecrated in front of Muslim prisoners. By his words and by his actions Bush repeatedly showed disrespect and intolerance for the Islamic faith.

Principle #6 states that a cowboy must help people in distress. One need only speak to the survivors of Hurricane Katrina in New Orleans to understand how Bush so thoroughly abrogated that responsibility. Principle #7 states that a cowboy must be a good worker. Today, leading Republicans criticize President Obama harshly whenever he takes a holiday to relax from the stresses of his job and plays golf. As of August, 2014 Obama had taken 125 days off as holidays. At the same point in his presidency Bush had taken 407 days off, a slacker at being president but consistently a slacker, having demonstrated the same characteristic of laziness in his university life at Yale and in his many failed business dealings as he did as president.

In regard to violation of the law, principle #9, author Michael Haas itemized 269 war crimes committed by Bush in his book "George W. Bush: War Criminal?" 3. Bush violated many international laws, including the UN charter, the Geneva conventions, protocols established at Nuremburg and even the American Constitution, thus violating with impunity rule #9 in Autry's code. The spying program that Bush initiated at NSA broke the law, as did his torture protocol and the process of "rendition" that he authorized through the CIA. Each time that Bush lied to Congress he broke the law, and there were many documented cases of blatant lies being told to Congress in the lead-up to the invasion of Iraq.

George Bush in his electoral campaigns portrayed himself as a self-confident, swaggering tough guy, modelling himself after the iconic image of an American cowboy, like John Wayne. He has in fact done nothing in his life to demonstrate any level of courage or bravery beyond ordering young men from families other than his own to go and die in a foreign war that had no legitimate purpose. His masculine toughness comes from his phoney cowboy costume, the teleprompter from which he reads his scripts, and from the artificial role that he played as 'Commander-in-Chief'. He has in fact led the life of a pampered dilettante, living off his family's money and his father's connections, yet portraying himself as some kind of brave warrior. His hypocrisy knew no bounds, surfacing repeatedly and most emphatically when he told a young soldier that he wished he could be on the ground in Iraq, taking part in combat. A noted draft-dodger who shirked his duty in Vietnam, and then shrugged off his responsibilities in the Texas National Reserve, Bush has at no point in his life shown any modicum of bravery or courage beyond sitting safely and securely in the Oval Office and delivering death and destruction to Iraq, and to America's young soldiers.

Most Americans relate positively to the historic image of the cowboy, an image that George Bush could not even come close to emulating. Although Bush has tried mightily to live up to this image of the iconic American cowboy, he is very much in the image of an artificial cowboy, carrying with him the paraphernalia and the hackneyed clichés, but lacking any of the core values. Such artificial pretense indicates a distinct lack of character, and more than one political observer commented on the lack of integrity of this president.

Christopher Hitchens was one journalist who helped define the Bush persona as a cowboy, and even came to support the war in Iraq. When Bush was still governor of Texas, but in the running to be the next president, Hitchens described him in these terms;

"George W. Bush is a man who is lucky to be governor of Texas. He is a man who is unusually incurious, abnormally unintelligent, amazingly inarticulate, fantastically uncultured, extraordinarily uneducated and apparently quite proud of all these things." 4.

Political journalist Rod Dreher, a Christian, a political conservative, contributor to the conservative National Review and long-time Republican supporter, said of the Bush presidency:

"As President Bush marched the country to war with Iraq, even some voices on the Right warned that this was a fool's errand. I dismissed them angrily. I thought them unpatriotic. But almost four years later I see that I was the fool. In Iraq this Republican president for whom I voted twice has shamed our country with weakness and incompetence. The fraud, the mendacity, the utter haplessness of our government's conduct of the Iraq war has been shattering to me. It wasn't supposed to turn out like this. Not under a Republican president." 5.

The incompetence of the Bush regime did not begin with the invasion of Iraq. At least three months before 9/11, German agents warned the CIA that Middle Eastern terrorists were planning to hijack commercial aircraft to use as weapons to attack important symbols of American culture. This warning was not even passed on to airline companies. Richard Clarke recounted over forty memos he sent to the Oval Office with the words "al Qaeda" in them, in the months leading up to 9/11, yet all of his requests for meetings with the president to discuss this urgent issue were rebuffed. Individual agents within the FBI reported about suspicious Arabs training to fly commercial jets in U.S. flying schools, but no action was taken. Bush received a briefing titled <u>Bin Laden Determined to Strike in U.S.</u> in August of 2001 but did not react in any way. NSA Director Michael Hayden said, "Throughout the summer of 2001 we had more than thirty warnings that something was imminent." With reference to terrorist messages that were intercepted, Porter J. Goss said, "The chatter level went way off the charts". On September 10, 2001, the day before 9/11, a message containing the phrase "Tomorrow is zero hour" and another saying "the match begins tomorrow" were received by NSA. Although both messages came from al Qaeda locations in Afghanistan, neither was translated until September 12, the day after the attacks on the twin towers. This incompetence was historic in the way that it opened the terrorist door to America for al Qaeda. **6.**

The Bush administration not only bungled the lead-up to 9/11 and the Iraq invasion as a response to 9/11, but also demonstrated supreme incompetence when dealing with the 9/11 Commission, established so that America could better understand and react to that disaster at home. Bush began by firmly opposing the formation of the 9/11 Commission, no doubt concerned that his incompetence, neglect, and mendacity, and his nefarious connections to Saudi Arabia, would be revealed in any detailed report about that national

COWBOY MOVIES & AMERICAN CULTURE

catastrophe. It was only with the perseverance of the families of 9/11 victims, and belatedly the support of Congress, that served to override the objections of the White House so that this investigation could be undertaken. Once this Commission was established, one would think that the Bush administration would be eager to facilitate its fact-finding. But Bush did everything in his power to restrict its range of options. He restricted access to his staff, restricted the format and the nature of the inquiry, and finally put restrictions on the release of information uncovered by the Commission. Twenty-eight pages of the final report were censored by the White House (redacted), many containing the words "Saudi Arabia". I wonder how many times the name "Prince Bandar bin Sultan" (aka Bandar Bush) was redacted from that document? Bush rejected outright a number of recommendations made by the commission, and generally showed contempt for the entire process. 7.

The incompetence of the Bush regime extended to the failed capture of bin Laden and his supporters, who were right there in Afghanistan, waiting to be taken. The Taliban government on two occasions offered to arrest bin Laden and his al Qaeda ringleaders, the first time to turn them over to a "third party" government, and the second time to turn them over directly to American authorities, if the United States government would provide proof that bin Laden was responsible for the 9/11 attacks. 8. This seemed a very reasonable request to most intelligent observers around the world, but on both occasions the Bush regime reacted to those proposals with scorn and rejected them. Bush then turned the capture of bin Laden into a debacle, waiting over two months to invade Afghanistan, not putting enough troops on the ground and eventually allowing bin Laden and his supporters to escape to the tribal regions of Pakistan.

It was only when Barrack Obama succeeded George Bush that bin Laden was finally found and assassinated. Given that every other al Qaeda operative was arrested and interrogated, it is extremely puzzling that Bin Laden was located and murdered, with his body being dumped at sea. One would think, on the basis of these actions, that more than one person in Washington was deathly afraid of bringing bin Laden to America and allowing him to talk. Given this paradox in procedure, it provides for interesting speculation as to what Osama bin Laden had to say, that would so terrify U.S. authorities.

Glenn Greenwald, in his book <u>A Tragic Legacy</u>, summarized the Bush presidency with these words:

"The Bush legacy is one whereby not only our moral standing but also our strength and security as a nation have been dangerously eroded. The president who venerated values of strength and subordinated all other goals to security has done more to diminish both than any modern American president. Machiavelli once argued that, among one's enemies it is better to be feared than to be loved, yet under the Bush presidency we are neither." **9.**

George Bush is an artificial cowboy, a pretense of the iconic American cowboy made famous by the urban cowboy, the Hollywood cowboy, the cowboy in country music, and the rodeo cowboy. That he used this phoney image to take America into a blood-thirsty and predatory war is a crime. It is a crime against America and its constitution and it is a crime against humanity.

CONCLUSION

"You can no more win a war than you can win an earthquake."

—JEANETTE RANKIN

Being in a perpetual state of war for the past 100 years has meant enormous profits for those already controlling most of the wealth in the United States and it has pushed the agenda in the White House by driving such fiascos as the invasion of Iraq. While young American soldiers are killed and crippled horribly by the technological nightmare that is modern warfare, America's rich become even richer through their ownership of the corporations that make the destructive machinery of war. Watching those huge missiles fly into Iraq, America's millionaires and billionaires must have gloated at the carnage as their shares in the military-industrial complex sky-rocketed. After all, it was not their children serving in Iraq, just as George Bush in a previous war was not serving in Vietnam. Over 21,000 new millionaires and billionaires were created in the United States alone during WW1. Imagine the number being created right now through this never-ending debacle in the Middle East, produced and directed by George Bush and Dick Cheney, and paid for by American taxpayers.

Few Americans saw these missiles launched into the heavily-populated city of Bagdad as a destructive force that was ripping apart the innocent bodies of Iraqi children. Many Americans saw "shock and awe" as this new video game war on their television screens every night, not as a force of evil that was destroying the homes and families of its innocent victims, splashing bloodshed and terror across the ancient city of Bagdad. While completely gutting the infrastructure of a country already reeling from a decade of inhuman sanctions, America created carnage in an act of aggression that is without parallel in its history. One soldier was quoted as saying, "We came in and we knew it wasn't going to be easy and…we shot everything that moved."

Americans followed the lead of their president and the sycophantic press, who identified Iraqis as "evil-doers", even as American soldiers were committing the most horrible and debasing acts of evil at Abu Ghraib prison, in Fallujah, in Tikrit, in Ramadi, at Guantanamo and across the entire country of Iraq. Using violence was a very natural and acceptable recourse for Americans when conflict existed, just as Americans use guns with total abandon against their family members, their fellow students and their work-mates. Bush reinforced the hackneyed cowboy phrase "We're the good guys. They're the bad guys" to unleash horror on Iraq that was never justified or in any way made to seem legitimate or justifiable. The revenge motive was strong for both American citizens after 9/11 and for George Bush personally after Saddam tried to assassinate his father.

So many corporations with close ties to Bush, Cheney and other White House power brokers made a fortune from the invasion of Iraq, including The Carlyle Group, General Electric, Halliburton, Blackwater, Shell, Exxon and General Dynamics. While working as Vice President, with the American people thinking he was working for them, Dick Cheney was continuing to draw a significant salary from Halliburton, estimated at over $200,000 a year, while holding over $10 million in Halliburton stock certificates. Promoting with great zeal the assault on Iraq had to be the absolute in both conflict of interest and total abandonment of ethical behavior when Cheney's favorite defense contractor, Halliburton, has earned over $50 billion from the war. **1.**

Richard A. Clarke worked in national security for 30 years, covering the terms of four presidents, from Reagan to George Bush. He was the National Coordinator for Security, Infrastructure Protection and Counter-Terrorism at the time of the 9/11 attacks, and was the only member of the Bush administration to apologize to the families of the victims of 9/11. He told a story in his book <u>Against All Enemies</u> about a Bangladeshi student he had in his law class at Columbia University. That student had watched Pakistani soldiers beat his father, and drag his mother out of their house. He said, "I am generally a non-violent man, but if I saw a Pakistani soldier today, I would kill him. You Americans should think about that, and about the long-term effect of what you have done to Iraq." **2.**

The next time an event like 9/11 takes place, Americans will no doubt call it "senseless violence", not thinking at all about that Bangladeshi student, and about how the invasion of Iraq has virtually guaranteed retaliation. Every bomb that is dropped in the Middle East creates 100 new terrorists willing to sacrifice their lives to rid their homeland of the mercenary invaders. Just as George Bush simplified a very complex issue by saying they hate our freedoms, our democracy and our liberty, so too does the media simplify a very complex rationale by calling the various terrorist assaults "senseless violence". When Muslims are being attacked in their homeland, are seeing their religion being denigrated, are seeing their countries being occupied and otherwise controlled by a western power that is obsessed with plundering their oil, then they will resort to any means necessary to deflect that power and exact retribution. Their actions in fighting back are in no way "senseless", and simply represent the only means available to defy the most futuristic, technologically-advanced war machine in history.

Richard Clarke in reacting to the invasion of Iraq said:

"I would like to see the United States return to being an inspiring role model, to helping others improve their quality of life—a nation known for real compassion and benevolence instead of an arrogant, threatening, military-industrial leviathan that inspires increasing revulsion, contempt, and fear from the world community." 3.

Sam Harris, in his book Letter to a Christian Nation, said more succinctly of the United States and Iraq;

"Our country now appears, as at no other time in her history, like a lumbering, bellicose, dim-witted giant. Anyone who cares about the fate of civilization would do well to recognize that the combination of great power and great stupidity is simply terrifying, even to one's friends." 4.

It was most terrifying to the many mothers and children and small babies and grandparents who were mercilessly slaughtered by this dim-witted giant, as the American military waged its unprovoked attack upon Iraq. Most Americans don't like to hear of their country being guilty of naked aggression. They like to think that their country, like the heroic cowboys of the Old West, only fights when its back is to the wall. They like to think that their country would never attack a country much smaller and much weaker than itself without provocation. Americans like to think that their country conducts its international obligations with honesty and integrity. This is the myth of America's greatness, a façade and a sham that exposes its dark side, corrupt with the wickedness of naked aggression.

The iconic cowboy image that evolved out of the cowboy culture of the western United States is considered by many to be the epitome of what it means to be American. Originally a synthesis of American and Hispanic culture, cowboy culture was defined not only by food, clothing, language and employment, but also by cultural values. The cowboy's relative isolation and work environment contributed to a unique set of frontier values that included self-reliance, individualism, hard work and heroism. Cowboys challenged villains, rescued women in distress, never took advantage of those weaker or incapable of defending themselves, and stood up for every noble cause, so that the myth of the cowboy paralleled the mythical qualities of the knights of medieval England.

George Bush was the cowboy president, resplendent in his cowboy accessories on the outside, but very much hollow and vacuous on the inside, where one might look in vain for a soul. He never lived up to the cowboy code set out by Gene Autry, and instead violated its essential tenets. His hypocrisy as a Christian knew no bounds. If there is indeed a heaven, he and his mercenary friends will never find it. He embarked on an odyssey that left both he and his regime as despotic war criminals and mass murderers, a posse of mendacious liars and prevaricators worthy only of a seat at the World Court in La Hague, accused of the war crimes that they committed against humanity.

Michael Haas said it best when he stated:

"Hundreds of years of human rights progress are in serious jeopardy as long as war criminals (like George Bush and Dick Cheney) live blissfully in the knowledge that they will never be held accountable for their crimes." **5.**

REFERENCE TEXTS

1. Bamford, James. <u>A Pretext for War</u>. Doubleday. 2004

2. Blum, William. <u>Killing Hope: US Military and CIA Interventions Since WWII</u>. Black Rose Books. 2003

3. Chomsky, Noam. <u>Failed States</u>. Metropolitan Books. 2006

4. Chomsky, Noam. <u>Hegemony or Survival</u> Metropolitan Books. 2003

5. Chomsky, Noam. <u>Power Systems</u>. Metropolitan Books. 2013

6. Chomsky, Noam. <u>The Essential Chomsky</u>. The New Press. 2008

7. Chomsky, Noam <u>Perilous Power</u> Paradigm Publishers 2007

7. Clark, Ramsey. <u>The Fire This Time: US War Crimes in the Gulf</u>. Thunder Mouth's Press. 1992

8. Clarke, Richard A. <u>Against All Enemies: Inside America's War on Terror</u>. Free Press. 2004

9. Dyer, Gwynne. <u>ISIS, Terror and Today's Middle East: Don't Panic</u>.

Random House Canada: 2015

10. Greenwald, Glenn. <u>A Tragic Legacy: How the Good vs Evil Mentality Destroyed the Bush Presidency</u>. Crown Publishers. 2007

11. Greenwald, Glenn <u>No Place to Hide</u> McClelland and Stewart 2014

12. Greenwald, Glenn <u>Great American Hypocrites</u> Three Rivers Press 2008

13. Haas, Michael. <u>George W. Bush; War Criminal?</u> Praeger Publishers 2009

14. Hine, Robert V. and John Faragher <u>Frontiers: A Short History of the American West</u>. Yale University Press 2007

15. Hunter, J. Marvin <u>The Trail Drivers of Texas</u> University of Texas Press 1985

16. Key, Joshua. <u>The Deserter's Tale</u> Atlantic Monthly Press. 2007

17. Lappe, Anthony and Marshall, Stephen. <u>True Lies</u> Penguin Group 2004

18. Loewen, James W. <u>Lies My Teacher Told Me</u>. Touchstone. 2007

19. McQuaig, Linda. <u>It's the Crude, Dude: War, Big Oil and the Fight for the Planet</u>. St. Martin's Press. 2007

20. Prados, John. <u>Hoodwinked: The Documents That Reveal How Bush Sold Us a War</u>. The New Press. 2004

21. Scoblic, J. Peter <u>Us vs Them</u> Viking-Penguin 2008

22. Slotkin, Richard. <u>Gunfighter Nation: The Myth of the Frontier in Twentieth Century America</u>. University of Oklahoma Press. 1992

23. Unger, Craig. <u>The Fall of the House of Bush</u> Scribner Press 2007

NOTES

Preface

1. Cost of War Project. Brown University. April 15, 2016

Chapter 1 Changing World Opinion

1. Richard Bernstein in The New York Times September 11, 2003

2. Noam Chomsky Hegemony or Survival Pg. 8 (Metropolitan Books 2003)

3. Gwynne Dyer. Isis, Terror and the Middle East. pg. 80

4. Ibid. pgs. 83-84

5. Martin Chulov in The Guardian Dec. 11, 2014

6. National Intelligence Council in a report to the CIA January, 2003

7. Glenn Greenwald A Tragic Legacy pg. 138 (Three Rivers Press, 2007)

8. CNN March 31, 2003

9. James Clapper speaking to AVSEC conference October 27, 2014

10. William Mayville press release from Pentagon September 23, 2014

11. Brendan Cole International Business Times Dec.8, 2015

12. Joshua Key. The Deserter's Tale. pgs. 105-106

13. Pete McMartin Vancouver Sun August 13, 2015 and

Jenny Euchi Vancouver Observer August, 2015

14. The Essential Chomsky pg. 379 Lies my Teacher Told Me Loewen pg. 273

15. Ibid. Loewen pg. 273

Chapter 2 A Penchant for Prevarication

1. James Bamford <u>A Pretext for War</u> pg. 325 (First Anchor Books 2004)

2. Ramsey Clark <u>The Fire This Time</u> pg. xxxi (Thunder's Mouth Press 2002)

3. Michael Gordon <u>New York Times</u> July 20, 2003

4. John Prados <u>Hoodwinked</u> pg. 5 (The NewPress 2004) Bamford pg. 268

5. Peter Scoblic <u>Us vs Them</u> pg. 210 (Viking Penguin 2008)

6. James W. Loewen Lies My Teacher Told Me pg. 273 (The New Press 2007)

7. Ibid. pgs 275/276

8. John Pilger <u>A New Pearl Harbor</u> The New Statesman December 16, 2002

9. Interview with Paul Reynolds BBC November 18, 1999

10. Op cit. Loewen pg.275

11.CBS News interview January 10, 2004 New York Times January 12, 2004.

12. Linda McQuaig <u>War, Big Oil and the Fight for the Planet</u> pg. 46

13. Op Cit. Loewen pg. 275

14. Ian Mayes <u>A Nasty Slip on Iraqi Oil</u> The Guardian June 7, 2003

15. Op Cit. Bamford pgs. 285-286

16. Ibid. Bamford pg. 286

17. Op Cit. Scoblic pg.219

18. Richard Clarke <u>Against All Enemies</u> pg. 231 (Simon and Schuster 2004)

19. Loewen pg. 414

20. Op Cit. Bamford pgs. 287-89

21. Ibid. Bamford pg. 289

22. Ibid. Bamford pg. 290

23. Ibid. Bamford pg. 290

24. Op Cit. Prados 295-297

25. Op Cit. Bamford pgs. 296-298

26. Ibid. pg. 316

27. Op Cit. Chomsky pg. 18

28. Ibid. pg. 18

29. Op Cit Bamford pg. 322

30. Noam Chomsky Failed States pg. 26 (Holt Paperbacks 2006)

31. Craig Unger The Fall of the House of Bush pg. 246

32. Op Cit. Prados pg.3

33. Op Cit. Loewen pg. 274-75

34. Op cit. McQuaig pg. 89

35. Op Cit. Prados pg. 1

36 Michael Getler The Sins of the Son Washington Post January 20, 2008

37. Sidney Blumenthal A State of Chaos The Guardian December 30, 2004

38. Steven Dougherty Hopes and Dreams pgs. 19-20 (Black Dog and Lewenthal Publishers 2008)

39. Op Cit. Bamford pg. 324

40. op Cit. Prados pg. 169

41. Scott Ritter speech given at St. Lawrence University. October 7, 2002

42. Op Cit. Scoblic pg. 216

43. Op Cit. Bamford pg. 307

44. Ibid. pgs. 301-306

45. Prados pg. 333

46. Marcia Kuntz: Andrew Seifter <u>Media Matters in America</u> September 24, 2004

47. Op Cit. Unger pg. 254

48. Op Cit. Bamford pg. 327-328

49. Ibid. Bamford pg. 330

50. Ibid. Bamford pg. 331

51. Op Cit. Prados pg. 105

52. Op Cit. Bamford pg. 370

53. Op Cit. Prados pg. 229-230

54. Op Cit. Bamford pgs. 296-297 and pgs. 323-326

55. Op Cit. Prados pg. 96

56. Ibid. pg. 103

57. Ibid. pg. 104

58. Op Cit. McQuaig pg. 59

59. Op Cit. McQuaig pg. 86 and Bamford pgs. 291-297

60. Jack Shafer, from Valeria Plame's book <u>Fair Game</u> pg. 232 Simon and Schuster 2007

61. David Lindorf <u>History Commons</u> website. July 25, 2003

62. Prados from Noam Chomsky's <u>Failed States</u> pg. 25

63. Ibid. Chomsky's <u>Failed States</u> pg. 21

64. Ibid. pg. 26

65. Op Cit. Prados pg. 15

66. Op Cit. Greenwald pg. 122

67. Op Cit. Chomsky Hegemony or Survival pg. 34 and pg. 130

68. Noam Chomsky The Toronto Star Dec. 21, 2003

69. Op Cit. Prados pg. 135

70. Glenn Kessler History Lesson: When Washington Looked the Other Way on Chemical Weapons Washington Post Sept. 4, 2013

Juan Cole U.S. Protected Iraq at U.N. from Iranian Charges of Chemical Weapons Use Informed Comment August 28, 2013

71. Op Cit. Prados pg. 135

72. Op Cit. Loewen pg. 274

73. Op Cit. Unger pg.12

74. Noam Chomsky Perilous Power pgs. 42-43 Paradigm Publishers 2007

75. Op Cit. Greenwald pg. xiii (preface)

76. Op Cit. Bamford pg. 335

77. Jonathon Freedlund Bush's Amazing Achievement The New York Review June 14, 2007

78. Jimmy Breslin Their Photos Tell the Story Newsday Dec. 30, 2003

79. Peter Johnson Media Mix Sept. 14, 2003

80. Op Cit. Unger pg. 256

81. Laurie Mylroie Very Awkward Facts Wall St. Journal April 2, 2004

82. Editors Richard Leone, Greg Anrig The War on our Freedoms pg. 248

83. Ken Auletta Fortress Bush The New Yorker Jan. 19, 2004

84. Greenwald, Glenn No Place to Hide McClelland and Stewart 2014

85. Op Cit. McQuaig. pgs. 59-60

86. Op Cit. Unger pgs. 256-257

Chapter 3 Cowboy Culture and its Influence on America

1. Robert Hine-John Faragher <u>Frontiers</u> pg. 14

2. Ibid. pg. 121

3. J. Marvin Hunter <u>The Trail Drivers of Texas</u>

4. Hine-Faragher. pg. 200

5. Michael Miller <u>The Quest to Bury the Old West</u> Washington Post Sept. 2015

6. Karen Dodwell <u>The Cowboy Myth, George Bush and the War with Iraq</u> Magazine Americana March, 2004

7. Susan Page <u>Gore Blasts Bush on Iraq War</u> USA Today Sept. 24, 2002

8. Elizabeth Bumiller <u>Bush, at NATO Meeting, Firms Up His Posse</u> New York Times Nov. 22, 2002

Chapter 4 Violence: Inherited from Cowboy Culture

1. Richard Slotkin <u>Gunfighter Nation: the Myth of the Frontier in Twentieth Century America</u> (University of Oklahoma Press 1998)

2. Op Cit. Prados pg. 49

3. Press release issued by National Research Council and Institute of Medicine May 6, 2013

4. Anthony Lappe and Stephen Marshall <u>True Lies</u> from National Crime Victimization Survey in 2011.

5. All incidents of violence gathered from a variety of internet sources, and from local newspapers and magazines.

6. Charles McCullogh <u>The Archetype of the Gun</u> Psychology and Business magazine Dec. 5, 2013

7. William Blum <u>williamblum.org/chapters/killing-hope/iraq</u>

8. Chomsky <u>Failed States</u> pg. 108

Chapter 5 The Good vs. Evil Mentality

1. Op Cit. Greenwald pgs 64 and pgs. 100-101

2. Ibid. pg. 56

3. Elizabeth Goitein <u>'Good Guys' and 'Bad Guys' in the War on Terror</u>

Al Jazeera America Dec. 9, 2013

4. Chris Hedges Collateral Damage TomDispatch.com June 3, 2008

5. Michael Haas <u>George W. Bush: War Criminal?</u> pg. 51 (Praeger Press 2009)

6. Ibid. pg. 51

7. Ibid. pgs. 75-76

8. Ibid. pg. 134

9. A Statement made by George W. Bush <u>News and Policies</u> June 26, 2003

10. Amber Ferguson and Adriane Usero <u>Remember: George W. Bush Said the U.S. Didn't Use Torture</u> The Huffington Post Sept. 12, 2014

11. Jane Mayer <u>A Deadly Interrogation</u> The New Yorker Nov. 14, 2005

12. Cathy Burke <u>Dick Cheney: CIA Techniques Post 9/11 'Absolutely Totally Justified'</u> Newsmax Dec. 8, 2014

13. Greenwald <u>Great American Hypocrites</u> (Three Rivers Press 2008) pgs. 110-111

14. Ibid. pgs. 229-230

15. Speech made by George W. Bush on board the USS Abraham Lincoln May 1, 2003

16. Op Cit. Chomsky Failed States pg. 48

17. Ibid. pg. 49

18. Ibid. pg.161

19. Ibid. pg. 50

20. Ibid. pg. 49

21. Joshua Key A Deserter's Tale pgs. 105-106 (House of Anansi Press 2007)

22. Ibid. pgs. 117-124

23. Ibid. pg. 109

24. Ibid. pg. 231

25. Op Cit. Chomsky Failed States pg. 66

26. Op Cit. Chomsky The Essential Chomsky pg. 379

Chapter 6 Manipulating and Abusing International Law

1. Daily Mail Report Invasion of Iraq Had No Legal Basis Jan. 12, 2010

2. Op Cit. Haas pgs. xi-xiii (preface)

3. Op. Cit. Chomsky Failed States pgs. 100-101

4. Richard Norton-Taylor War Resignation Letter Censored The Guardian March 24, 2005

5. Noam Chomsky Dominance and its Dilemmas Boston Review Oct. 2003

6. Op. Cit. Chomsky Failed States pg. 100

7. Op. Cit. Haas pg. 5

8. Op. Cit. Greenwald A Tragic Legacy pg. 163

9. Op. Cit. Haas pg.4

10. Cathy Burke Newsmax.com Dec. 8, 2014

11. Op. Cit. Haas pg. xii (preface)

12. Op. Cit. Loewen pg. 278

13. Op Cit. Unger pg. 3

14. Ibid. pg. 14

15 Ibid. pg. 4

16. Ibid. pg. 130

17. Noam Chomsky The Essential Chomsky pg. 386 (The New Press 2008)

18. Press Freedom Index 2004-2006 Reporters Without Borders

19. Op. Cit. Chomsky Failed States pg. 3

20. Op. Cit. Norton-Taylor Nov. 18, 2008

21. Op. Cit. Chomsky Failed States pg. 67

22. Ramsey Clark The Fire This Time: U.S. War Crimes in the Gulf

(Thunder's Mouth Press 1992)

23. Ibid. pg. 47

24. Ibid. pgs. 70-71

25. William Blum Killing Hope pgs. 64-70 (Black Rose Books 1998)

26. Ibid. pg. 64

27. Ibid. pgs. 64-65

28. Ibid. pgs. 64-72

29. Ibid. pgs. 121-215

30. Ibid. pg. 214

31. Op. Cit. Loewen pg. 265

32. Ibid. pg. 266

33. Ibid. 266

34. Ibid. pgs. 266-267

35. Op. Cit. Haas pgs. 69, 147, 157, 160, 163 and 235.

36. Charles H. Ferguson documentary Inside Job (2010)

37. Op. Cit. Hine-Faragher pg. 131

Chapter 7 Revenge

1. Tamar Lewin Sihk Owner of Gas Station Fatally Shot in Rampage New York Times Sept. 17, 2001

2. Margaret Talbot The Story of a Hate Crime The New Yorker June 22, 2015

3. Op. Cit. Bamford pg. 255

4. Frontline Jan. 1991 and April, 1993 at pbs.org

5. Bob Woodward at rt.com Dec. 18, 2008

6. Charles Lewis The Lies We Believe About Iraq June 23, 2014 at billmoyers.com

Chapter 8 Money: The Predominant Goal in Life

1. Peter Beaumont and Joanna Walters <u>Greenspan Admits Iraq Was About Oil, As Deaths Put at 1.2m</u> The Guardian Sept. 16, 2007

2. Lonnie Shoultz <u>The Army's New Car is a Lemon</u> 2003 militarycorruption.com

3. Robert Greenwald and Derrick Crowe <u>No Success in Iraq- Unless You're a War Profiteer</u> The Huffington Post Dec. 15, 2011

4. Michael D. Yeats (editor) <u>More Unequal: Aspects of Class in the United States</u>

pg. 40 (Monthly Review Press 2007)

5. Op. Cit. Loewen pgs. 225-226

6. Ibid. pg. 275

7. Eisenhower Speech presented by NPR staff Jan. 17, 2011 <u>Ike's Warning of Military Expansion</u>

8. Eisenhower Farewell Speech from the White House. Jan. 17, 1961

9. Pope Francis speech in USA Nov. 20, 2015 Yahoo News

Chapter 9 The Fallout from Iraq

1. Op. Cit. Scolbic pg. 179

2. Ibid. pg. 181

3. Ibid. pg. 180

4. Ibid. pgs. 178-181

5. Ibid. pgs. 182-183

6. Op. Cit. Chomsky Failed States pg. 70

7. Ibid. pg. 30

8. Speech by George W. Bush, Milwaukee, Wis., Oct. 3, 2003

9. Dwight D. Eisenhower's Military-Industrial Speech 1961

coursesa.matrix.msu.edu/~hst306/documents/indust.html

10. Op. Cit. Chomsky Failed States pg. 78

11. Ibid. pg. 78

Chapter 10 Is George W. Bush a Real Cowboy?

1. Holly George-Warren Public Cowboy #1: The Life and Times of Gene Autry
Oxford University Press June 28, 2011

2. From Gene Autry's Survivors Trust, printed in Delta Airlines Magazine
Aug. 1998

3. Op. Cit. Haas

4. From "Quotes about George Bush" Angel Fire

5. Op. Cit. Greenwald A Tragic Legacy pg. 33

6. Op. Cit. Loewen pg. 270

7. Ibid. pg. 271

8. Ibid. pg. 271

9. Op. Cit. Greenwald A Tragic Legacy pg. 284

Conclusion

1. Op. Cit. Loewen pgs. 174-175

2. Op. Cit. Clarke Against All Enemies

3. Ibid. Clarke

4. Sam Harris Letter to a Christian Nation pg. xi (preface)

5. Op. Cit. Haas pg. xvi (preface)